Let's Keep in Touch

Follow Us

Online

Visit US at

www.EffortlessMath.com

https://www.facebook.com/Effortlessmath

https://goo.gl/2B6qWW

Online Math Lessons

It's easy! Here's how it works.

1- Request a FREE introductory session.

2- Meet a Math tutor online.

3- Start Learning Math in Minutes.

Send Email to: **info@EffortlessMath.com**

www.EffortlessMath.com

… So Much More Online!

- **FREE Math lessons**

- **More Math learning books!**

- **Online Math Tutors**

Looking for an Online Math Tutor?

Need a PDF format of this book?

Send Email to: info@EffortlessMath.com

SSAT UPPER LEVEL Math

in

7 Days

Step–By–Step Guide to Preparing for the SSAT UPPER LEVEL Math Test Quickly

By

Reza Nazari & Ava Ross

Copyright © 2018

Reza Nazari & Ava Ross

All inquiries should be addressed to:

info@effortlessMath.com

www.EffortlessMath.com

ISBN-13: 978-1723019180

ISBN-10: 1723019186

Published by: Effortless Math Education

www.EffortlessMath.com

Description

The goal of this book is simple. It will help students incorporate the best method and the right strategies to prepare for the SSAT Upper Level Math FAST and EFFECTIVELY.

SSAT UPPER LEVEL Math in 7 Days is full of specific and detailed material that will be key to succeeding on the SSAT Upper Level Mathematics section. It's filled with the critical math concepts a student will need in order to ace the test. Math concepts in this book break down the topics, so the material can be quickly grasped. Examples are worked step–by–step, so you learn exactly what to do.

SSAT UPPER LEVEL Math in 7 Days helps students to focus on all Math topics that they will need to prepare for the SSAT Upper Level Math test. Students only need to spend about 4 – 6 hours daily in their 7–day period in order to be well prepared for the test. This book with 2 complete SSAT Upper Level Mathematics tests is all a student will ever need to fully prepare for the SSAT Upper Level Math.

This workbook includes practice test questions. It contains easy–to–read essential summaries that highlight the key areas of the SSAT Upper Level Mathematics test. Effortless Math test study guide reviews the most important components of the SSAT Upper Level Mathematics test. Anyone planning to take the SSAT Upper Level test should take advantage of the review material and practice test questions contained in this study guide.

Whether your student is intimidated by math, or even if he or she was the first to raise their hand in the Math classes, this book can help them accelerate the learning process and put them on the right track.

Inside the pages of this workbook, students can learn basic math operations in a structured manner with a complete study program to help them understand essential math skills. It also has many exciting features, including:

- Dynamic design and easy–to–follow activities
- Step–by–step guide for all Math topics

- Targeted, skill–building practices
- A fun, interactive and concrete learning process
- Math topics are grouped by category, so you can focus on the topics you struggle on
- All solutions for the exercises are included, so you will always find the answers
- 2 Complete SSAT Upper Level Math Practice Tests that reflect the format and question types on SSAT Upper Level

SSAT UPPER LEVEL Math in 7 Days is a breakthrough in Math learning — offering a winning formula and the most powerful methods for learning basic Math topics confidently. Each section offers step–by–step instruction and helpful hints, with a few topics being tackled each day. Two complete REAL SSAT Upper Level Mathematics tests are provided at the back of the book to refine students' Math skills.

Effortlessly and confidently follow the step–by–step instructions in this book to prepare for the SSAT Upper Level Mathematics in a short period of time.

SSAT UPPER LEVEL *Math in 7 Days* is the only book your student will ever need to master Basic Math topics! It can be used as a self–study course – you do not need to work with a Math tutor. (It can also be used with a Math tutor).

You'll be surprised how fast your student masters the Math topics covering on SSAT UPPER LEVEL Mathematics Test.

Ideal for self–study as well as for classroom usage.

About the Author

Reza Nazari is the author of more than 100 Math learning books including:
– **Math and Critical Thinking Challenges:** For the Middle and High School Student
– **ISEE UPPER LEVEL Math in 30 Days**
– **ASVAB Math Workbook 2018 – 2019**
– **Effortless Math Education Workbooks**
– **and many more Mathematics books …**

Reza is also an experienced Math instructor and a test–prep expert who has been tutoring students since 2008. Reza is the founder of Effortless Math Education, a tutoring company that has helped many students raise their standardized test scores—and attend the colleges of their dreams. Reza provides an individualized custom learning plan and the personalized attention that makes a difference in how students view math.

To ask questions about Math, you can contact Reza via email at:
reza@EffortlessMath.com

Find Reza's professional profile at:
goo.gl/zoC9rJ

Contents

Day 1: Fundamentals and Building Blocks

Math Topics that you'll learn today:

✓ Place Value

✓ Rounding

✓ Whole Number Addition and Subtraction

✓ Whole Number Multiplication and Division

✓ Rounding and Estimates

✓ Comparing Numbers

✓ Simplifying Fractions

✓ Adding and Subtracting Fractions

✓ Multiplying and Dividing Fractions

✓ Adding Mixed Numbers

✓ Subtracting Mixed Numbers

✓ Multiplying Mixed Numbers

✓ Dividing Mixed Numbers

✓ Comparing Decimals

✓ Rounding Decimals

✓ Adding and Subtracting Decimals

✓ Multiplying and Dividing Decimals

✓ Converting Between Fractions, Decimals and Mixed Numbers

"If people do not believe that mathematics is simple, it is only because they do not realize how complicated life is." — John von Neumann

---

Place Value

| *Helpful* *Hints* | The value of the place, or position, of a digit in a number.
For the number 3,684.26 | **Example:**
In 456, the 5 is in "tens" position. |

Decimal Place Value Chart

Millions	Hundred thousands	Ten thousands	Thousands	Hundreds	Tens	Ones	Decimal point	Tenths	Hundredths	Thousandths	Ten-thousandths	Hundred thousandths	Millionths
			3	6	8	4	.	2	6				

✍ **Write each number in expanded form.**

1) Thirty–five $30 + 5$

2) Sixty–seven   ___ + ___

3) Forty–two   ___ + ___

4) Eighty–nine   ___ + ___

5) Ninety–one   ___ + ___

✍ **Circle the correct one.**

6) The 2 in 72 is in the   ones place   tens place   hundreds place

7) The 6 in 65 is in the   ones place   tens place   hundreds place

8) The 2 in 342 is in the   ones place   tens place   hundreds place

9) The 5 in 450 is in the   ones place   tens place   hundreds place

10) The 3 in 321 is in the   ones place   tens place   hundreds place

---

Rounding

Helpful *Hints*	– Rounding is putting a number up or down to the nearest whole number or the nearest hundred, etc.	Example: 64 rounded to the nearest ten is 60, because 64 is closer to 60 than to 70.

✎*Round each number to the underlined place value.*

1) 9̲72

2) 2,9̲95

3) 36̲4

4) 8̲1

5) 5̲5

6) 33̲4

7) 1,2̲03

8) 9.5̲7

9) 7.4̲84

10) 9.1̲4

11) 3̲9

12) 9̲,123

13) 3,45̲2

14) 5̲69

15) 1,2̲30

16) 9̲8

17) 9̲3

18) 3̲7

19) 49̲3

20) 2,9̲23

21) 9̲,845

22) 55̲5

23) 9̲39

24) 6̲9

Whole Number Addition and Subtraction

Helpful	1– Line up the numbers.	**Example:**
	2– Start with the unit place. (ones place)	231 + 120 = 351
Hints	3– Regroup if necessary.	292 – 90 = 202
	4– Add or subtract the tens place.	
	5– Continue with other digits.	

✏ *Solve.*

1) A school had 891 students last year. If all last year students and 338 new students have registered for this year, how many students will there be in total?

2) Alice has just started her first job after graduating from college. Her yearly income is $33,000 per year. Alice's father income is $56,000 per year and her mother's income is $49,000. What is yearly income of Alice and her parent altogether?

3) Tom had $895 dollars in his saving account. He gave $235 dollars to his sister, Lisa. How much money does he have left?

4) Emily has 830 marbles, Daniel has 970 marbles, and Ethan has 230 marbles less than Daniel. How many marbles do they have in all?

✏ *Find the missing number.*

5) 890 – .... = 300

6) 1000 – .... = 200

7) .... – 4000 = 92000

8) 60000 – 51000 = ...

9) 3400 – .... = 3200

10) 33000 – 5000 = ...

Whole Number Multiplication and Division

Helpful *Hints*	**Multiplication:**	**Example:**
	– Learn the times tables first!	$200 \times 90 = 18,000$
	– For multiplication, line up the numbers you are multiplying.	
	– Start with the ones place.	$18,000 \div 90 = 200$
	– Continue with other digits	
	– A typical division problem:	
	Dividend ÷ Divisor = Quotient	
	Division:	
	– In division, we want to find how many times a number (divisor) is contained in another number (dividend).	
	– The result in a division problem is the quotient.	

✎**Multiply and divided.**

1) $340 \div 8 =$

2) $1800 \div 20 =$

3) $50000 \div 10 =$

4) $966 \div 30 =$

5) $201 \times 20 =$

6) $400 \times 50 =$

7) $400 \times 90 =$

8) $888 \times 90 =$

9) $80 \times 80 =$

10) $122 \times 12 =$

11) $609 \times 8 =$

12) $220 \times 12 =$

13) A group of 235 students has collected $8,565 for charity during last month. They decided to split the money evenly among 5 charities. How much will each charity receive?

14) Maria and her two brothers have 9 boxes of crayons. Each box contains 56 crayons. How many crayons do Maria and her two brothers have?

Rounding and Estimates

Helpful Hints	– Rounding and estimating are math strategies used for approximating a number. – To estimate means to make a rough guess or calculation. – To round means to simplify a known number by scaling it slightly up or down.	**Example:** $73 + 69 \approx 140$

✎ *Estimate the sum by rounding each added to the nearest ten.*

1) 55 + 9

2) 25 + 12

3) 83 + 7

4) 32 + 37

5) 13 + 74

6) 34 + 11

7) 39 + 77

8) 25 + 4

9) 61 + 73

10) 64 + 59

11) 14 + 68

12) 82 + 12

13) 43 + 66

14) 45 + 65

15) 553 + 232

16) 418 + 846

17) 582 + 277

18) 2771 + 1651

19) 7436 + 3575

20) 1542 + 8738

21) 3843 + 6579

22) 4722 + 8186

23) 2419 + 7224

24) 6768 + 3169

Comparing Numbers

Helpful Hints	Comparing:	Example:
	Equal to =	
	Less than <	56 > 35
	Greater than >	
	Greater than or equal ≥	
	Less than or equal ≤	

✎*Use > = <.*

1) 35   67

2) 89   56

3) 56   35

4) 27   56

5) 34   34

6) 28   45

7) 89   67

8) 90   56

9) 94   98

10) 48   23

11) 24   54

12) 89   89

13) 50   30

14) 20   20

✎*Use less than, equal to or greater than.*

15) 23 _____ 34

16) 89 _____ 98

17) 45 _____ 25

18) 34 _____ 32

19) 91 _____ 91

20) 57 _____ 55

21) 85 _____ 78

22) 56 _____ 43

23) 34 _____ 34

24) 92 _____ 98

25) 38 _____ 46

26) 67 _____ 58

27) 88 _____ 69

28) 23 _____ 34

Simplifying Fractions

Helpful	– Evenly divide both the top and bottom of the fraction by 2, 3, 5, 7, … etc. – Continue until you can't go any further.	Example:
Hints		$\frac{4}{12} = \frac{2}{6} = \frac{1}{3}$

✍ *Simplify the fractions.*

1) $\frac{22}{36}$

2) $\frac{8}{10}$

3) $\frac{12}{18}$

4) $\frac{6}{8}$

5) $\frac{13}{39}$

6) $\frac{5}{20}$

7) $\frac{16}{36}$

8) $\frac{18}{36}$

9) $\frac{20}{50}$

10) $\frac{6}{54}$

11) $\frac{45}{81}$

12) $\frac{21}{28}$

13) $\frac{35}{56}$

14) $\frac{52}{64}$

15) $\frac{13}{65}$

16) $\frac{44}{77}$

17) $\frac{21}{42}$

18) $\frac{15}{36}$

19) $\frac{9}{24}$

20) $\frac{20}{80}$

21) $\frac{25}{45}$

Adding and Subtracting Fractions

Helpful Hints	– For "like" fractions (fractions with the same denominator), add or subtract the numerators and write the answer over the common denominator. – Find equivalent fractions with the same denominator before you can add or subtract fractions with different denominators. – Adding and Subtracting with the same denominator:

$$\frac{a}{b} + \frac{c}{b} = \frac{a+c}{b}$$
$$\frac{a}{b} - \frac{c}{b} = \frac{a-c}{b}$$

– Adding and Subtracting fractions with different denominators:

$$\frac{a}{b} + \frac{c}{d} = \frac{ad+cb}{bd}$$
$$\frac{a}{b} - \frac{c}{d} = \frac{ad-cb}{bd}$$

✎ Add fractions.

1) $\frac{2}{3} + \frac{1}{2}$ 4) $\frac{7}{4} + \frac{5}{9}$ 7) $\frac{3}{4} + \frac{2}{5}$

2) $\frac{3}{5} + \frac{1}{3}$ 5) $\frac{2}{5} + \frac{1}{5}$ 8) $\frac{2}{3} + \frac{1}{5}$

3) $\frac{5}{6} + \frac{1}{2}$ 6) $\frac{3}{7} + \frac{1}{2}$ 9) $\frac{16}{25} + \frac{3}{5}$

✎ Subtract fractions.

10) $\frac{4}{5} - \frac{2}{5}$ 13) $\frac{8}{9} - \frac{3}{5}$ 16) $\frac{3}{4} - \frac{13}{18}$

11) $\frac{3}{5} - \frac{2}{7}$ 14) $\frac{3}{7} - \frac{3}{14}$ 17) $\frac{5}{8} - \frac{2}{5}$

12) $\frac{1}{2} - \frac{1}{3}$ 15) $\frac{4}{15} - \frac{1}{10}$ 18) $\frac{1}{2} - \frac{1}{9}$

Multiplying and Dividing Fractions

Helpful Hints	– **Multiplying fractions:** multiply the top numbers and multiply the bottom numbers. – **Dividing fractions:** Keep, Change, Flip Keep first fraction, change division sign to multiplication, and flip the numerator and denominator of the second fraction. Then, solve!	**Example:** $$\frac{a}{b} \times \frac{c}{d} = \frac{a \times c}{b \times d}$$ $$\frac{a}{b} \div \frac{c}{d} = \frac{a}{b} \times \frac{d}{c} = \frac{ad}{bc}$$

✎ *Multiplying fractions. Then simplify.*

1) $\dfrac{1}{5} \times \dfrac{2}{3}$

2) $\dfrac{3}{4} \times \dfrac{2}{3}$

3) $\dfrac{2}{5} \times \dfrac{3}{7}$

4) $\dfrac{3}{8} \times \dfrac{1}{3}$

5) $\dfrac{3}{5} \times \dfrac{2}{5}$

6) $\dfrac{7}{9} \times \dfrac{1}{3}$

7) $\dfrac{2}{3} \times \dfrac{3}{8}$

8) $\dfrac{1}{4} \times \dfrac{1}{3}$

9) $\dfrac{5}{7} \times \dfrac{7}{12}$

✎ *Dividing fractions.*

10) $\dfrac{2}{9} \div \dfrac{1}{4}$

11) $\dfrac{1}{2} \div \dfrac{1}{3}$

12) $\dfrac{6}{11} \div \dfrac{3}{4}$

13) $\dfrac{11}{14} \div \dfrac{1}{10}$

14) $\dfrac{3}{5} \div \dfrac{5}{9}$

15) $\dfrac{1}{2} \div \dfrac{1}{2}$

16) $\dfrac{3}{5} \div \dfrac{1}{5}$

17) $\dfrac{12}{21} \div \dfrac{3}{7}$

18) $\dfrac{5}{14} \div \dfrac{9}{10}$

Adding Mixed Numbers

Helpful Hints	Use the following steps for both adding and subtracting mixed numbers.	Example:
	– Find the Least Common Denominator (LCD) – Find the equivalent fractions for each mixed number. – Add fractions after finding common denominator. – Write your answer in lowest terms.	$1\frac{3}{4} + 2\frac{3}{8} = 4\frac{1}{8}$

✎*Add.*

1) $4\frac{1}{2} + 5\frac{1}{2}$

2) $2\frac{3}{8} + 3\frac{1}{8}$

3) $6\frac{1}{5} + 3\frac{2}{5}$

4) $1\frac{1}{3} + 2\frac{2}{3}$

5) $5\frac{1}{6} + 5\frac{1}{2}$

6) $3\frac{1}{3} + 1\frac{1}{3}$

7) $1\frac{10}{11} + 1\frac{1}{3}$

8) $2\frac{3}{6} + 1\frac{1}{2}$

9) $5\frac{3}{5} + 5\frac{1}{5}$

10) $7 + \frac{1}{5}$

11) $1\frac{5}{7} + \frac{1}{3}$

12) $2\frac{1}{4} + 1\frac{1}{2}$

Subtract Mixed Numbers

Helpful

Hints

Use the following steps for both adding and subtracting mixed numbers.

Find the Least Common Denominator (LCD)
– Find the equivalent fractions for each mixed number.
– Add or subtract fractions after finding common denominator.
– Write your answer in lowest terms.

Example:

$$5\frac{2}{3} - 3\frac{2}{7} = 2\frac{8}{21}$$

✎**Subtract.**

1) $4\frac{1}{2} - 3\frac{1}{2}$

2) $3\frac{3}{8} - 3\frac{1}{8}$

3) $6\frac{3}{5} - 5\frac{1}{5}$

4) $2\frac{1}{3} - 1\frac{2}{3}$

5) $6\frac{1}{6} - 5\frac{1}{2}$

6) $3\frac{1}{3} - 1\frac{1}{3}$

7) $2\frac{10}{11} - 1\frac{1}{3}$

8) $2\frac{1}{2} - 1\frac{1}{2}$

9) $6\frac{3}{5} - 2\frac{1}{5}$

10) $7\frac{2}{5} - 1\frac{1}{5}$

11) $2\frac{5}{7} - 1\frac{1}{3}$

12) $2\frac{1}{4} - 1\frac{1}{2}$

Multiplying Mixed Numbers

Helpful *Hints*	1- Convert the mixed numbers to improper fractions. 2- Multiply fractions and simplify if necessary. $$a\frac{c}{b} = a + \frac{c}{b} = \frac{ab \quad c}{b}$$	**Example:** $$2\frac{1}{3} \times 5\frac{3}{7} =$$ $$\frac{7}{3} \times \frac{38}{7} = \frac{38}{3} = 12\frac{2}{3}$$

✎ *Find each product.*

1) $1\frac{2}{3} \times 1\frac{1}{4}$

2) $1\frac{3}{5} \times 1\frac{2}{3}$

3) $1\frac{2}{3} \times 3\frac{2}{7}$

4) $4\frac{1}{8} \times 1\frac{2}{5}$

5) $2\frac{2}{5} \times 3\frac{1}{5}$

6) $1\frac{1}{3} \times 1\frac{2}{3}$

7) $1\frac{5}{8} \times 2\frac{1}{2}$

8) $3\frac{2}{5} \times 2\frac{1}{5}$

9) $2\frac{2}{3} \times 4\frac{1}{4}$

10) $2\frac{3}{5} \times 1\frac{2}{4}$

11) $1\frac{1}{3} \times 1\frac{1}{4}$

12) $3\frac{2}{5} \times 1\frac{1}{5}$

Dividing Mixed Numbers

Helpful	1- Convert the mixed numbers to improper fractions.	**Example:**
Hints	2- Divide fractions and simplify if necessary.	$2\frac{1}{3} \times 5\frac{3}{7} =$

$$a\frac{c}{b} = a + \frac{c}{b} = \frac{ab+c}{b}$$

$$\frac{7}{3} \times \frac{38}{7} = \frac{38}{3} = 12\frac{2}{3}$$

✎ *Find each quotient.*

1) $2\frac{1}{5} \div 2\frac{1}{2}$

2) $2\frac{3}{5} \div 1\frac{1}{3}$

3) $3\frac{1}{6} \div 4\frac{2}{3}$

4) $1\frac{2}{3} \div 3\frac{1}{3}$

5) $4\frac{1}{8} \div 2\frac{2}{4}$

6) $3\frac{1}{2} \div 2\frac{3}{5}$

7) $3\frac{5}{9} \div 1\frac{2}{5}$

8) $2\frac{2}{7} \div 1\frac{1}{2}$

9) $3\frac{1}{5} \div 1\frac{1}{2}$

10) $4\frac{3}{5} \div 2\frac{1}{3}$

11) $6\frac{1}{6} \div 1\frac{2}{3}$

12) $2\frac{2}{3} \div 1\frac{1}{3}$

Comparing Decimals

Helpful		**Decimals:** is a fraction written in a special form. For example, instead of writing $\frac{1}{2}$ you can write 0.5.	**Example:**
Hints	-	**For comparing:**	$2.67 > 0.267$
		Equal to =	
		Less than <	
		Greater than >	
		Greater than or equal ≥	
		Less than or equal ≤	

✍ *Write the correct comparison symbol (>, < or =).*

1) 1.25   2.3

2) 0.5   0.23

3) 3.2   3.2

4) 4.58   45.8

5) 2.75   0.275

6) 5.2   5

7) 3.1   0.31

8) 6.33   0.733

9) 8   0.8

10) 4.56   0.456

11) 1.12   1.14

12) 2.77   2.78

13) 6.08   6.11

14) 1.11   0.211

15) 2.6   2.55

16) 1.24   1.25

17) 5.52   0.552

18) 0.33   0.033

19) 14.4   14.4

20) 0.05   0.50

21) 0.59   0.7

22) 0.5   0.05

23) 0.90   0.9

24) 0.27   0.4

Rounding Decimals

Helpful Hints	We can round decimals to a certain accuracy or number of decimal places. This is used to make calculation easier to do and results easier to understand, when exact values are not too important. First, you'll need to remember your place values:	**Example:** 6.37 = 6

12.4567

1: tens   2: ones   4: tenths

5: hundredths   6: thousandths   7: tens thousandths

✎ *Round each decimal number to the nearest place indicated.*

1) 0.23

2) 4.04

3) 5.623

4) 0.266

5) 6.37

6) 0.88

7) 8.24

8) 7.0760

9) 1.629

10) 6.3959

11) 1.9

12) 5.2167

13) 5.863

14) 8.54

15) 80.69

16) 65.85

17) 70.78

18) 615.755

19) 16.4

20) 95.81

21) 2.408

22) 76.3

23) 116.514

24) 8.06

Adding and Subtracting Decimals

Helpful Hints	1– Line up the numbers.	Example:
	2– Add zeros to have same number of digits for both numbers.	16.18
	3– Add or Subtract using column addition or subtraction.	− 13.45
		2.73

✎ **Add and subtract decimals.**

1) 15.14
    − 12.18
    _____

2) 65.72
    + 43.67
    _____

3) 82.56
    + 12.28
    _____

4) 34.18
    − 23.45
    _____

5) 90.37
    + 56.97
    _____

6) 45.78
    − 23.39
    _____

✎ **Solve.**

7) ____ + 1.3 = 4.8

8) 4.2 + ____ = 11.6

9) 9.9 + ____ = 16

10) 6.9 + ____ = 16.4

11) ____ + 5.1 = 8.6

12) ____ + 7.9 = 15.2

Multiplying and Dividing Decimals

Helpful *Hints*	**For Multiplication:** – Set up and multiply the numbers as you do with whole numbers. – Count the total number of decimal places in both of the factors. – Place the decimal point in the product. **For Division:** – If the divisor is not a whole number, move decimal point to right to make it a whole number. Do the same for dividend. – Divide similar to whole numbers.

✎ *Find each product.*

1)
$$
\begin{array}{r}
4.5 \\
\times\ 1.6 \\
\hline
\end{array}
$$

4)
$$
\begin{array}{r}
8.9 \\
\times\ 9.7 \\
\hline
\end{array}
$$

7)
$$
\begin{array}{r}
5.7 \\
\times\ 7.8 \\
\hline
\end{array}
$$

2)
$$
\begin{array}{r}
7.7 \\
\times\ 9.9 \\
\hline
\end{array}
$$

5)
$$
\begin{array}{r}
15.1 \\
\times\ 12.6 \\
\hline
\end{array}
$$

8)
$$
\begin{array}{r}
98.20 \\
\times\ 100 \\
\hline
\end{array}
$$

3)
$$
\begin{array}{r}
2.6 \\
\times\ 1.5 \\
\hline
\end{array}
$$

6)
$$
\begin{array}{r}
6.9 \\
\times\ 3.3 \\
\hline
\end{array}
$$

9)
$$
\begin{array}{r}
23.99 \\
\times\ 1000 \\
\hline
\end{array}
$$

✎ *Find each quotient.*

10) $9.2 \div 3.6$

11) $27.6 \div 3.8$

12) $12.6 \div 4.7$

13) $6.5 \div 8.1$

14) $1.4 \div 10$

15) $3.6 \div 100$

16) $4.24 \div 10$

17) $14.6 \div 100$

18) $1.8 \div 1000$

Converting Between Fractions, Decimals and Mixed Numbers

Helpful

Hints

Fraction to Decimal:

– Divide the top number by the bottom number.

Decimal to Fraction:

– Write decimal over 1.

– Multiply both top and bottom by 10 for every digit on the right side of the decimal point.

– Simplify.

✎ **Convert fractions to decimals.**

1) $\frac{9}{10}$

2) $\frac{56}{100}$

3) $\frac{3}{4}$

4) $\frac{2}{5}$

5) $\frac{3}{9}$

6) $\frac{40}{50}$

7) $\frac{12}{10}$

8) $\frac{8}{5}$

9) $\frac{69}{10}$

✎ **Convert decimal into fraction or mixed numbers.**

10) 0.3

11) 4.5

12) 2.5

13) 2.3

14) 0.8

15) 0.25

16) 0.14

17) 0.2

18) 0.08

19) 0.45

20) 2.6

21) 5.2

Answers of Worksheets – Day 1

Place Value

1) 30 + 5
2) 60 + 7
3) 40 + 2
4) 80 + 9

5) 90 + 1
6) ones place
7) tens place
8) ones place

9) tens place
10) hundreds place

Rounding

1) 1000
2) 3000
3) 360
4) 80
5) 60
6) 330
7) 1200
8) 9.6

9) 7.5
10) 9.1
11) 40
12) 9000
13) 3,450
14) 600
15) 1,200
16) 100

17) 90
18) 40
19) 490
20) 2,900
21) 10,000
22) 560
23) 900
24) 70

Whole Number Addition and Subtraction

1) 1229
2) 138000
3) 660
4) 2540

5) 590
6) 800
7) 96000
8) 9000

9) 200
10) 28000

Whole Number Multiplication and Division

1) 42.5
2) 90
3) 5000
4) 32.2
5) 4020

6) 20000
7) 36000
8) 79920
9) 6400
10) 1464

11) 4872
12) 2640
13) 1713
14) 504

Rounding and Estimates

1) 70	7) 120	13) 110	19) 11020
2) 40	8) 30	14) 120	20) 10280
3) 90	9) 130	15) 780	21) 10420
4) 70	10) 120	16) 1270	22) 12910
5) 37	11) 80	17) 860	23) 9640
6) 40	12) 90	18) 4420	24) 9940

Comparing Numbers

1) 35 < 67	11) 24 < 54	21) 85 greater than 78
2) 89 > 56	12) 89 = 89	22) 56 greater than 43
3) 56 > 35	13) 50 > 30	23) 34 equal to 34
4) 27< 56	14) 20 = 20	24) 92 less than 98
5) 34 = 34	15) 23 less than 34	25) 38 less than 46
6) 28 < 45	16) 89 less than 98	26) 67 greater than 58
7) 89 > 67	17) 45 greater than 25	27) 88 greater than 69
8) 90 > 56	18) 34 greater than 32	28) 23 less than 34
9) 94 < 98	19) 91 equal to 91	
10) 48 > 23	20) 57 greater than 55	

Simplifying Fractions

1) $\frac{11}{18}$	6) $\frac{1}{4}$	11) $\frac{5}{9}$
2) $\frac{4}{5}$	7) $\frac{4}{9}$	12) $\frac{3}{4}$
3) $\frac{2}{3}$	8) $\frac{1}{2}$	13) $\frac{5}{8}$
4) $\frac{3}{4}$	9) $\frac{2}{5}$	14) $\frac{13}{16}$
5) $\frac{1}{3}$	10) $\frac{1}{9}$	15) $\frac{1}{5}$

16) $\frac{4}{7}$ 18) $\frac{5}{12}$ 20) $\frac{1}{4}$

17) $\frac{1}{2}$ 19) $\frac{3}{8}$ 21) $\frac{5}{9}$

Adding and Subtracting Fractions

1) $\frac{7}{6}$ 7) $\frac{23}{20}$ 13) $\frac{13}{45}$

2) $\frac{14}{15}$ 8) $\frac{13}{15}$ 14) $\frac{3}{14}$

3) $\frac{4}{3}$ 9) $\frac{31}{25}$ 15) $\frac{1}{6}$

4) $\frac{83}{36}$ 10) $\frac{2}{5}$ 16) $\frac{1}{36}$

5) $\frac{3}{5}$ 11) $\frac{11}{35}$ 17) $\frac{9}{40}$

6) $\frac{13}{14}$ 12) $\frac{1}{6}$ 18) $\frac{7}{18}$

Multiplying and Dividing Fractions

1) $\frac{2}{15}$ 7) $\frac{1}{4}$ 13) $\frac{55}{7}$

2) $\frac{1}{2}$ 8) $\frac{1}{12}$ 14) $\frac{27}{25}$

3) $\frac{6}{35}$ 9) $\frac{5}{12}$ 15) 1

4) $\frac{1}{8}$ 10) $\frac{8}{9}$ 16) 3

5) $\frac{6}{25}$ 11) $\frac{3}{2}$ 17) $\frac{4}{3}$

6) $\frac{7}{27}$ 12) $\frac{8}{11}$ 18) $\frac{25}{63}$

Adding Mixed Numbers

1) 10

2) $5\frac{1}{2}$

3) $9\frac{3}{5}$

4) 4

5) $10\frac{2}{3}$

6) $4\frac{2}{3}$

7) $3\frac{8}{33}$

8) 4

9) $10\frac{4}{5}$

10) $7\frac{1}{5}$

11) $2\frac{1}{21}$

12) $3\frac{3}{4}$

Subtract Mixed Numbers

1) 1

2) $\frac{1}{4}$

3) $1\frac{2}{5}$

4) $\frac{2}{3}$

5) $\frac{2}{3}$

6) 2

7) $1\frac{19}{33}$

8) 1

9) $4\frac{2}{5}$

10) $6\frac{1}{5}$

11) $1\frac{8}{21}$

12) $\frac{3}{4}$

Multiplying Mixed Numbers

1) $2\frac{1}{12}$

2) $2\frac{2}{3}$

3) $5\frac{10}{21}$

4) $5\frac{31}{40}$

5) $7\frac{17}{25}$

6) $2\frac{2}{9}$

7) $4\frac{1}{16}$

8) $7\frac{12}{25}$

9) $11\frac{1}{3}$

10) $3\frac{9}{10}$

11) $1\frac{2}{3}$

12) $4\frac{2}{25}$

Dividing Mixed Numbers

1) $\frac{22}{25}$

2) $1\frac{19}{20}$

3) $\frac{19}{28}$

4) $\frac{1}{2}$

5) $1\frac{13}{20}$

6) $1\frac{9}{26}$

7) $2\frac{34}{63}$ 9) $2\frac{2}{15}$ 11) $3\frac{7}{10}$

8) $1\frac{11}{21}$ 10) $1\frac{34}{35}$ 12) 2

Comparing Decimals

1) 1.25 < 2.3   13) 6.08 < 6.11
2) 0.5 > 0.23   14) 1.11 > 0.211
3) 3.2 = 3.2   15) 2.6 > 2.55
4) 4.58 < 45.8   16) 1.24 < 1.25
5) 2.75 > 0.275   17) 5.52 > 0.552
6) 5.2 > 5   18) 0.33 > 0.033
7) 3.1 > 0.31   19) 14.4 = 14.4
8) 6.33 > 0.733   20) 0.05 < 0.50
9) 8 > 0.8   21) 0.59 < 0.7
10) 4.56 > 0.456   22) 0.5 > 0.05
11) 1.12 < 1.14   23) 0.90 = 0.9
12) 2.77 < 2.78   24) 0.27 < 0.4

Rounding Decimals

1) 0.2   9) 1.63   17) 70.8
2) 4.0   10) 6.4   18) 616
3) 5.6   11) 2   19) 16
4) 0.3   12) 5   20) 96
5) 6   13) 5.9   21) 2
6) 0.9   14) 8.5   22) 76
7) 8.2   15) 81   23) 116.5
8) 7   16) 66   24) 8.1

Adding and Subtracting Decimals

1) 2.96

2) 109.39

3) 94.84

4) 10.73

5) 147.34

6) 22.39

7) 3.5

8) 7.4

9) 6.1

10) 9.5

11) 3.5

12) 7.3

Multiplying and Dividing Decimals

1) 7.2

2) 76.23

3) 3.9

4) 86.33

5) 190.26

6) 22.77

7) 44.46

8) 9820

9) 23990

10) 2.5555...

11) 7.2631...

12) 2.6808...

13) 0.8024...

14) 0.14

15) 0.036

16) 0.424

17) 0.146

18) 0.0018

Converting Between Fractions, Decimals and Mixed Numbers

1) 0.9

2) 0.56

3) 0.75

4) 0.4

5) 0.333...

6) 0.8

7) 1.2

8) 1.6

9) 6.9

10) $\frac{3}{10}$

11) $4\frac{1}{2}$

12) $2\frac{1}{2}$

13) $2\frac{3}{10}$

14) $\frac{4}{5}$

15) $\frac{1}{4}$

16) $\frac{7}{50}$

17) $\frac{1}{5}$

18) $\frac{2}{25}$

19) $\frac{9}{20}$

20) $2\frac{3}{5}$

21) $5\frac{1}{5}$

Day 2: Integers and Order of Operations

Math Topics that you'll learn today:

- ✓ Divisibility Rules
- ✓ Factoring Numbers
- ✓ Greatest Common Factor
- ✓ Least Common Multiple
- ✓ Adding and Subtracting Integers
- ✓ Multiplying and Dividing Integers
- ✓ Ordering Integers and Numbers
- ✓ Arrange, Order, and Comparing Integers
- ✓ Order of Operations
- ✓ Mixed Integer Computations
- ✓ Integers and Absolute Value
- ✓ Writing Ratios
- ✓ Simplifying Ratios

"Wherever there is number, there is beauty." –Proclus

Divisibility Rules

Helpful	-	Divisibility means that a number can be divided by other numbers evenly.	**Example:**
Hints			24 is divisible by 6, because 24 ÷ 6 = 4

✍ **Use the divisibility rules to find the factors of each number.**

       8   <u>2</u> 3 <u>4</u> 5 6 7 <u>8</u> 9 10

1) 16   2 3 4 5 6 7 8 9 10

2) 10   2 3 4 5 6 7 8 9 10

3) 15   2 3 4 5 6 7 8 9 10

4) 28   2 3 4 5 6 7 8 9 10

5) 36   2 3 4 5 6 7 8 9 10

6) 15   2 3 4 5 6 7 8 9 10

7) 27   2 3 4 5 6 7 8 9 10

8) 70   2 3 4 5 6 7 8 9 10

9) 57   2 3 4 5 6 7 8 9 10

10) 102   2 3 4 5 6 7 8 9 10

11) 144   2 3 4 5 6 7 8 9 10

12) 75   2 3 4 5 6 7 8 9 10

Factoring Numbers

Helpful		Example:
	- Factoring numbers means to break the numbers into their prime factors.	
Hints	- First few prime numbers: 2, 3, 5, 7, 11, 13, 17, 19	$12 = 2 \times 2 \times 3$

✍ **List all positive factors of each number.**

1) 68	6) 78	11) 54
2) 56	7) 50	12) 28
3) 24	8) 98	13) 55
4) 40	9) 45	14) 85
5) 86	10) 26	15) 48

✍ **List the prime factorization for each number.**

16) 50	19) 21	22) 26
17) 25	20) 45	23) 86
18) 69	21) 68	24) 93

Greatest Common Factor

Helpful	- List the prime factors of each number. - Multiply common prime factors.	**Example:**
Hints		$200 = 2 \times 2 \times 2 \times 5 \times 5$ $60 = 2 \times 2 \times 3 \times 5$ GCF $(200, 60) = 2 \times 2 \times 5 = 20$

✍ *Find the GCF for each number pair.*

1) 20, 30

2) 4, 14

3) 5, 45

4) 68, 12

5) 5, 12

6) 15, 27

7) 3, 24

8) 34, 6

9) 4, 10

10) 5, 3

11) 6, 16

12) 30, 3

13) 24, 28

14) 70, 10

15) 45, 8

16) 90, 35

17) 78, 34

18) 55, 75

19) 60, 72

20) 100, 78

21) 30, 40

Least Common Multiple

Helpful	- Find the GCF for the two numbers. - Divide that GCF into either number. - Take that answer and multiply it by the other number.	**Example:** LCM (200, 60): GCF is 20 $200 \div 20 = 10$ $10 \times 60 = 600$
Hints		

✎ *Find the LCM for each number pair.*

1) 4, 14

2) 5, 15

3) 16, 10

4) 4, 34

5) 8, 3

6) 12, 24

7) 9, 18

8) 5, 6

9) 8, 19

10) 9, 21

11) 19, 29

12) 7, 6

13) 25, 6

14) 4, 8

15) 30, 10, 50

16) 18, 36, 27

17) 12, 8, 18

18) 8, 18, 4

19) 26, 20, 30

20) 10, 4, 24

21) 15, 30, 45

Adding and Subtracting Integers

Helpful	-	**Integers:** {… , −3, −2, −1, 0, 1, 2, 3, …} Includes: zero, counting numbers, and the negative of the counting numbers.	**Example:**
		− Add a positive integer by moving to the right on the number line.	$12 + 10 = 22$ $25 − 13 = 12$
Hints		− Add a negative integer by moving to the left on the number line.	$(−24) + 12 = −12$
			$(−14) + (−12) = −26$
		− Subtract an integer by adding its opposite.	$14 − (−13) = 27$

✎Find the sum.

1) $(− 12) + (− 4)$

2) $5 + (− 24)$

3) $(− 14) + 23$

4) $(− 8) + (39)$

5) $43 + (−12)$

6) $(− 23) + (− 4) + 3$

7) $4 + (− 12) + (− 10) + (− 25)$

8) $19 + (− 15) + 25 + 11$

9) $(− 9) + (− 12) + (32 − 14)$

10) $4 + (− 30) + (45 − 34)$

✎Find the difference.

11) $(− 14) − (− 9) − (18)$

12) $(− 9) − (− 25)$

13) $(− 12) − (8)$

14) $(28) − (− 4)$

15) $(34) − (2)$

16) $(55) − (− 5) + (− 4)$

17) $(9) − (2) − (− 5)$

18) $(2) − (4) − (− 15)$

19) $(23) − (4) − (− 34)$

20) $(− 45) − (− 87)$

Multiplying and Dividing Integers

Helpful	(negative) × (negative) = positive	Examples:
	(negative) ÷ (negative) = positive	$3 \times 2 = 6$
Hints	(negative) × (positive) = negative	$3 \times -3 = -9$
	(negative) ÷ (positive) = negative	$-2 \times -2 = 4$
	(positive) × (positive) = positive	$10 \div 2 = 5$
		$-4 \div 2 = -2$
		$-12 \div -6 = 3$

✍ **Find each product.**

1) $(-8) \times (-2)$ 6) $10 \times (-5)$

2) 3×6 7) 8×8

3) $(-4) \times 5 \times (-6)$ 8) $(-8) \times (-9)$

4) $2 \times (-6) \times (-6)$ 9) $6 \times (-5) \times 3$

5) $11 \times (-12)$ 10) $6 \times (-1) \times 2$

✍ **Find each quotient.**

11) $18 \div 3$ 16) $(-66) \div (-11)$

12) $(-24) \div 4$ 17) $64 \div 8$

13) $(-63) \div (-9)$ 18) $(-121) \div 11$

14) $54 \div 9$ 19) $72 \div 9$

15) $20 \div (-2)$ 20) $16 \div 4$

Ordering Integers and Numbers

Helpful *Hints*	To compare numbers, you can use number line! As you move from left to right on the number line, you find a bigger number!	**Example:** Order integers from least to greatest. $(-11, -13, 7, -2, 12)$ $-13 < -11 < -2 < 7 < 12$

✎ **Order each set of integers from least to greatest.**

1) $-15, -19, 20, -4, 1$ ___, ___, ___, ___, ___, ___

2) $6, -5, 4, -3, 2$ ___, ___, ___, ___, ___, ___

3) $15, -42, 19, 0, -22$ ___, ___, ___, ___, ___, ___

4) $26, -91, 0, -13, 67, -55$ ___, ___, ___, ___, ___, ___

5) $-17, -71, 90, -25, -54, -39$ ___, ___, ___, ___, ___, ___

6) $98, 5, 46, 19, 77, 24$ ___, ___, ___, ___, ___, ___

✎ **Order each set of integers from greatest to least.**

7) $-2, 5, -3, 6, -4$ ___, ___, ___, ___, ___, ___

8) $-37, 7, -17, 27, 47$ ___, ___, ___, ___, ___, ___

9) $32, -27, 19, -17, 15$ ___, ___, ___, ___, ___, ___

10) $68, 81, 21, -18, 94, 72$ ___, ___, ___, ___, ___, ___

Arrange, Order, and Comparing Integers

Helpful *Hints*	When using a number line, numbers increase as you move to the right.	**Examples:** $5 < 7,$ $-5 < -2$ $-18 < -12$

✍ *Arrange these integers in descending order.*

1) $21, 71, -18, -10, 82$ ___, ___, ___, ___, ___, ___

2) $15, 11, 20, 12, -9, -5$ ___, ___, ___, ___, ___, ___

3) $-5, 20, 15, 9, -11$ ___, ___, ___, ___, ___, ___

4) $19, 18, -9, -6, -11$ ___, ___, ___, ___, ___, ___

5) $56, -34, -12, -5, 32$ ___, ___, ___, ___, ___, ___

✍ *Compare. Use >, =, <*

6) -8 ____ 12

7) -10 ____ -16

8) 43 ____ 34

9) 15 ____ -16

10) -354 ____ -345

11) -56 ____ -58

12) 78 ____ 87

13) -92 ____ -102

14) -12 ____ -12

15) -721 ____ -821

Order of Operations

Helpful	-	Use "order of operations" rule when there are more than one math operation.	**Example:**
Hints	-	PEMDAS (parentheses / exponents / multiply / divide / add / subtract)	$(12 + 4) \div (-4) = -4$

✎ *Evaluate each expression.*

1) $(2 \times 2) + 5$

2) $24 - (3 \times 3)$

3) $(6 \times 4) + 8$

4) $25 - (4 \times 2)$

5) $(6 \times 5) + 3$

6) $64 - (2 \times 4)$

7) $25 + (1 \times 8)$

8) $(6 \times 7) + 7$

9) $48 \div (4 + 4)$

10) $(7 + 11) \div (-2)$

11) $9 + (2 \times 5) + 10$

12) $(5 + 8) \times \frac{3}{5} + 2$

13) $2 \times 7 - (\frac{10}{9 - 4})$

14) $(12 + 2 - 5) \times 7 - 1$

15) $(\frac{7}{5 - 1}) \times (2 + 6) \times 2$

16) $20 \div (4 - (10 - 8))$

17) $\frac{50}{4(5 - 4) - 3}$

18) $2 + (8 \times 2)$

Mixed Integer Computations

Helpful	It worth remembering:	Example:
Helpful	(negative) × (negative) = positive	
Hints	(negative) ÷ (negative) = positive	(−5) + 6 = 1
	(negative) × (positive) = negative	(−3) × (−2) = 6
	(negative) ÷ (positive) = negative	(9) ÷ (−3) = − 3
	(positive) × (positive) = positive	

✎ *Compute.*

1) $(-70) \div (-5)$

2) $(-14) \times 3$

3) $(-4) \times (-15)$

4) $(-65) \div 5$

5) $18 \times (-7)$

6) $(-12) \times (-2)$

7) $\dfrac{(-60)}{(-20)}$

8) $24 \div (-8)$

9) $22 \div (-11)$

10) $\dfrac{(-27)}{3}$

11) $4 \times (-4)$

12) $\dfrac{(-48)}{12}$

13) $(-14) \times (-2)$

14) $(-7) \times (7)$

15) $\dfrac{-30}{-6}$

16) $(-54) \div 6$

17) $(-60) \div (-5)$

18) $(-7) \times (-12)$

19) $(-14) \times 5$

20) $88 \div (-8)$

Integers and Absolute Value

Helpful	To find an absolute value of a number, just find it's distance from 0!	Example:
Hints		$\|-6\| = 6$
		$\|6\| = 6$
		$\|-12\| = 12$
		$\|12\| = 12$

✎ Write absolute value of each number.

1) − 4

2) − 7

3) − 8

4) 4

5) 5

6) − 10

7) 1

8) 6

9) 8

10) − 2

11) − 1

12) 10

13) 3

14) 7

15) − 5

16) − 3

17) − 9

18) 2

19) 4

20) − 6

21) 9

✎ Evaluate.

22) $\|-43\| - \|12\| + 10$

23) $76 + \|-15 - 45\| - \|3\|$

24) $30 + \|-62\| - 46$

25) $\|32\| - \|-78\| + 90$

26) $\|-35 + 4\| + 6 - 4$

27) $\|-4\| + \|-11\|$

28) $\|-6 + 3 - 4\| + \|7 + 7\|$

29) $\|-9\| + \|-19\| - 5$

Writing Ratios

Helpful	− A ratio is a comparison of two numbers. Ratio **Example:** can be written as a division.
Hints	$3:5$, or $\frac{3}{5}$

✎ **Express each ratio as a rate and unite rate.**

1) 120 miles on 4 gallons of gas.

2) 24 dollars for 6 books.

3) 200 miles on 14 gallons of gas

4) 24 inches of snow in 8 hours

✎ **Express each ratio as a fraction in the simplest form.**

5) 3 feet out of 30 feet

6) 18 cakes out of 42 cakes

7) 16 dimes t0 24 dimes

8) 12 dimes out of 48 coins

9) 14 cups to 84 cups

10) 45 gallons to 65 gallons

11) 10 miles out of 40 miles

12) 22 blue cars out of 55 cars

13) 32 pennies to 300 pennies

14) 24 beetles out of 86 insects

Simplifying Ratios

Helpful	– You can calculate equivalent ratios by multiplying or dividing both sides of the ratio by the same number.	**Examples:**
Hints		$3 : 6 = 1 : 2$
		$4 : 9 = 8 : 18$

✎ *Reduce each ratio.*

1) $21 : 49$

2) $20 : 40$

3) $10 : 50$

4) $14 : 18$

5) $45 : 27$

6) $49 : 21$

7) $100 : 10$

8) $12 : 8$

9) $35 : 45$

10) $8 : 20$

11) $25 : 35$

12) $21 : 27$

13) $52 : 82$

14) $12 : 36$

15) $24 : 3$

16) $15 : 30$

17) $3 : 36$

18) $8 : 16$

19) $6 : 100$

20) $2 : 20$

21) $10 : 60$

22) $14 : 63$

23) $68 : 80$

24) $8 : 80$

Answers of Worksheets – Day 2

Divisibility Rules

1) 16   <u>2</u> 3 <u>4</u> 5 6 7 <u>8</u> 9 10

2) 10   <u>2</u> 3 4 <u>5</u> 6 7 8 9 <u>10</u>

3) 15   2 <u>3</u> 4 <u>5</u> 6 7 8 9 10

4) 28   <u>2</u> 3 <u>4</u> 5 6 <u>7</u> 8 9 10

5) 36   <u>2</u> <u>3</u> <u>4</u> 5 <u>6</u> 7 8 <u>9</u> 10

6) 18   <u>2</u> <u>3</u> 4 5 <u>6</u> 7 8 <u>9</u> 10

7) 27   2 <u>3</u> 4 5 6 7 8 <u>9</u> 10

8) 70   <u>2</u> 3 4 <u>5</u> 6 <u>7</u> 8 9 <u>10</u>

9) 57   2 <u>3</u> 4 5 6 7 8 9 10

10) 102   <u>2</u> <u>3</u> 4 5 <u>6</u> 7 8 9 10

11) 144   <u>2</u> <u>3</u> <u>4</u> 5 <u>6</u> 7 <u>8</u> <u>9</u> 10

12) 75   2 <u>3</u> 4 <u>5</u> 6 7 8 9 10

Factoring Numbers

1) 1, 2, 4, 17, 34, 68
2) 1, 2, 4, 7, 8, 14, 28, 56
3) 1, 2, 3, 4, 6, 8, 12, 24
4) 1, 2, 4, 5, 8, 10, 20, 40
5) 1, 2, 43, 86
6) 1, 2, 3, 6, 13, 26, 39, 78
7) 1, 2, 5, 10, 25, 50
8) 1, 2, 7, 14, 49, 98
9) 1, 3, 5, 9, 15, 45
10) 1, 2, 13, 26
11) 1, 2, 3, 6, 9, 18, 27, 54
12) 1, 2, 4, 7, 14, 28

13) 1, 5, 11, 55
14) 1, 5, 17, 85
15) 1, 2, 3, 4, 6, 8, 12, 16, 24, 48
16) $2 \times 5 \times 5$
17) 5×5
18) 3×23
19) 3×7
20) $3 \times 3 \times 5$
21) $2 \times 2 \times 17$
22) 2×13
23) 2×43
24) 3×31

Greatest Common Factor

1) 10
2) 2
3) 5
4) 4
5) 1
6) 3
7) 3
8) 2
9) 2
10) 1
11) 2
12) 3
13) 4
14) 10
15) 1
16) 5
17) 2
18) 5
19) 12
20) 2
21) 10

Least Common Multiple

1) 28
2) 15
3) 80
4) 68
5) 24
6) 24
7) 18
8) 30
9) 152
10) 63
11) 551
12) 42
13) 150
14) 8
15) 150
16) 108
17) 72
18) 72
19) 780
20) 120
21) 90

Adding and Subtracting Integers

1) − 16
2) − 19
3) 9
4) 31
5) 31
6) − 24
7) − 43
8) 40
9) − 3
10) − 15
11) − 23
12) 16
13) − 20
14) 32
15) 32
16) 56
17) 12
18) 13
19) 53
20) 42

Multiplying and Dividing Integers

1) 16
2) 18
3) 120
4) 72
5) − 132
6) − 50
7) 64
8) 72
9) − 90

10) – 12   14) 6   18) – 11

11) 6   15) – 10   19) 8

12) – 6   16) 6   20) 4

13) 7   17) 8

Ordering Integers and Numbers

1) – 19, – 15, – 4, 1, 20   6) 5, 19, 24, 46, 77, 98

2) – 5, – 3, 2, 4, 6   7) 6, 5, – 2, – 3, – 4

3) – 42, – 22, 0, 15, 19   8) 47, 27, 7, – 17, – 37

4) – 91, – 55, – 13, 0, 26, 67   9) 32, 19, 15, – 17, – 27

5) – 71, – 54, – 39, – 25, – 17, 90   10) 94, 81, 72, 68, 21, – 18

Arrange and Order, Comparing Integers

1) 82, 71, 21, – 10, – 18

2) 20, 15, 12, 11, – 5, – 9

3) 20, 15, 9, – 5, –11

4) 19, 18, – 6, – 9, – 11

5) 56, 32, – 5, – 12, – 34

6) <   10) <   14) =

7) >   11) >   15) >

8) >   12) <

9) >   13) >

Order of Operations

1) 9   7) 33   13) 12

2) 15   8) 49   14) 62

3) 32   9) 6   15) 28

4) 17   10) – 9   16) 10

5) 33   11) 29   17) 50

6) 56   12) 9.8   18) 18

Mixed Integer Computations

1) 14
2) − 42
3) 60
4) − 13
5) − 126
6) 24
7) 3
8) − 3
9) − 2
10) − 9
11) − 16
12) − 4
13) 28
14) − 49
15) 5
16) − 9
17) 12
18) 84
19) − 70
20) − 11

Integers and Absolute Value

1) 4
2) 7
3) 8
4) 4
5) 5
6) 10
7) 1
8) 6
9) 8
10) 2
11) 1
12) 10
13) 3
14) 7
15) 5
16) 3
17) 9
18) 2
19) 4
20) 6
21) 9
22) 41
23) 133
24) 46
25) 44
26) 33
27) 15
28) 21
29) 23

Writing Ratios

1) $\frac{120\ miles}{4\ gallons}$, 30 miles per gallon

2) $\frac{24\ dollars}{6\ books}$, 4.00 dollars per book

3) $\frac{200\ miles}{14\ gallons}$, 14.29 miles per gallon

4) $\frac{24"\ of\ snow}{8\ hours}$, 3 inches of snow per hour

5) $\frac{1}{10}$

6) $\frac{3}{7}$

7) $\frac{2}{3}$

8) $\frac{1}{4}$

9) $\frac{1}{6}$

10) $\frac{9}{13}$

11) $\frac{1}{4}$

12) $\frac{2}{5}$

13) $\frac{8}{75}$

14) $\dfrac{12}{43}$

Simplifying Ratios

1) 3 : 7

2) 1 : 2

3) 1 : 5

4) 7 : 9

5) 5 : 3

6) 7 : 3

7) 10 : 1

8) 3 : 2

9) 7 : 9

10) 2 : 5

11) 5 : 7

12) 7 : 9

13) 26 : 41

14) 1 : 3

15) 8 : 1

16) 1 : 2

17) 1 : 12

18) 1 : 2

19) 3 : 50

20) 1 : 10

21) 1 : 6

22) 2 : 9

23) 17 : 20

24) 1 : 10

Day 3: Proportions and Variables

Math Topics that you'll learn today:

- ✓ Create a Proportion
- ✓ Similar Figures
- ✓ Simple and Compound Interest
- ✓ Ratio and Rates Word Problems
- ✓ Percentage Calculations
- ✓ Table of Common Percent
- ✓ Converting Between Percent, Fractions, and Decimals
- ✓ Percent Problems
- ✓ Markup, Discount, and Tax
- ✓ Expressions and Variables
- ✓ Simplifying Variable Expressions
- ✓ Simplifying Polynomial Expressions
- ✓ Translate Phrases into an Algebraic Statement

"Do not worry about your difficulties in mathematics. I can assure you mine are still greater." – Albert Einstein

Create a Proportion

Helpful	– A proportion contains 2 equal fractions! A proportion simply means that two fractions are equal.	**Example:**
Hints		2, 4, 8, 16
		$\dfrac{2}{4} = \dfrac{8}{16}$

✎ *Create proportion from the given set of numbers.*

1) 1, 6, 2, 3

2) 12, 144, 1, 12

3) 16, 4, 8, 2

4) 9, 5, 27, 15

5) 7, 10, 60, 42

6) 8, 7, 24, 21

7) 10, 5, 8, 4

8) 3, 12, 8, 2

9) 2, 2, 1, 4

10) 3, 6, 7, 14

11) 2, 6, 5, 15

12) 7, 2, 14, 4

Similar Figures

Helpful	– Two or more figures are similar if the corresponding angles are equal, and the corresponding sides are in proportion.	**Example:**
Hints		3–4–5 triangle is similar to a 6–8–10 triangle

✎*Each pair of figures is similar. Find the missing side.*

1)

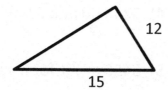 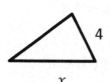

2)

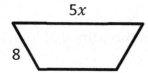 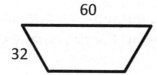

3)

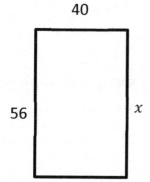 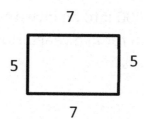

Simple Interest

| **Helpful**

Hints | **Simple Interest:** The charge for borrowing money or the return for lending it.
Interest = principal x rate x time

$$I = prt$$ | **Example:**

$450 at 7% for 8 years.

$$I = prt$$

$$I = 450 \times 0.07 \times 8 = \$252 =$$ |

✎ **Use simple interest to find the ending balance.**

1) $1,300 at 5% for 6 years.

2) $5,400 at 7.5% for 6 months.

3) $25,600 at 9.2% for 5 years

4) $24,000 at 8.5% for 9 years.

5) $450 at 7% for 8 years.

6) $54,200 at 8% for 5 years.

7) $240 interest is earned on a principal of $1500 at a simple interest rate of 4% interest per year. For how many years was the principal invested?

8) A new car, valued at $28,000, depreciates at 9% per year from original price. Find the value of the car 3 years after purchase.

9) Sara puts $2,000 into an investment yielding 5% annual simple interest; she left the money in for five years. How much interest does Sara get at the end of those five years?

Ratio and Rates Word Problems

Helpful *Hints*	To solve a ratio or a rate word problem, create a proportion and use cross multiplication method!	**Example:** $\frac{x}{4} = \frac{8}{16}$ $16x = 4 \times 8$ $x = 2$

✎ *Solve.*

1) In a party, 10 soft drinks are required for every 12 guests. If there are 252 guests, how many soft drink is required?

2) In Jack's class, 18 of the students are tall and 10 are short. In Michael's class 54 students are tall and 30 students are short. Which class has a higher ratio of tall to short students?

3) Are these ratios equivalent?

   12 cards to 72 animals 11 marbles to 66 marbles

4) The price of 3 apples at the Quick Market is $1.44. The price of 5 of the same apples at Walmart is $2.50. Which place is the better buy?

5) The bakers at a Bakery can make 160 bagels in 4 hours. How many bagels can they bake in 16 hours? What is that rate per hour?

6) You can buy 5 cans of green beans at a supermarket for $3.40. How much does it cost to buy 35 cans of green beans?

Percentage Calculations

Helpful	-	Use the following formula to find part, whole, or percent:	Example:
Hints		$\text{part} = \dfrac{\text{percent}}{100} \times \text{whole}$	$\dfrac{20}{100} \times 100 = 20$

✎ **Calculate the percentages.**

1) 50% of 25

2) 80% of 15

3) 30% of 34

4) 70% of 45

5) 10% of 0

6) 80% of 22

7) 65% of 8

8) 78% of 54

9) 50% of 80

10) 20% of 10

11) 40% of 40

12) 90% of 0

13) 20% of 70

14) 55% of 60

15) 80% of 10

16) 20% of 880

17) 70% of 100

18) 80% of 90

✎ **Solve.**

19) 50 is what percentage of 75?

20) What percentage of 100 is 70

21) Find what percentage of 60 is 35.

22) 40 is what percentage of 80?

Converting Between Percent, Fractions, and Decimals

Helpful	– To a percent: Move the decimal point 2 places to the right and add the % symbol. **Examples:**
Hints	– Divide by 100 to convert a number from percent to decimal. 30% = 0.3
	0.24 = 24%

✍ Converting fractions to decimals.

1) $\dfrac{50}{100}$ 4) $\dfrac{80}{100}$ 7) $\dfrac{90}{100}$

2) $\dfrac{38}{100}$ 5) $\dfrac{7}{100}$ 8) $\dfrac{20}{100}$

3) $\dfrac{15}{100}$ 6) $\dfrac{35}{100}$ 9) $\dfrac{7}{100}$

✍ Write each decimal as a percent.

10) 0.5   13) 0.524   16) 3.63

11) 0.9   14) 0.1   17) 0.008

12) 0.002   15) 0.03   18) 4.78

Percent Problems

Helpful	Base = Part ÷ Percent	Example:
	Part = Percent × Base	2 is 10% of 20.
Hints	Percent = Part ÷ Base	2 ÷ 0.10 = 20
		2 = 0.10 × 20
		0.10 = 2 ÷ 20

✎ *Solve each problem.*

1) 51 is 340% of what?

2) 93% of what number is 97?

3) 27% of 142 is what number?

4) What percent of 125 is 29.3?

5) 60 is what percent of 126?

6) 67 is 67% of what?

7) 67 is 13% of what?

8) 41% of 78 is what?

9) 1 is what percent of 52.6?

10) What is 59% of 14 m?

11) What is 90% of 130 inches?

12) 16 inches is 35% of what?

13) 90% of 54.4 hours is what?

14) What percent of 33.5 is 21?

15) Liam scored 22 out of 30 marks in Algebra, 35 out of 40 marks in science and 89 out of 100 marks in mathematics. In which subject his percentage of marks in best?

16) Ella require 50% to pass. If she gets 280 marks and falls short by 20 marks, what were the maximum marks she could have got?

Markup, Discount, and Tax

Helpful

Hints

- **Markup** = selling price – cost
  Markup rate = markup divided by the cost

- **Discount:**
  Multiply the regular price by the rate of discount

  Selling price =

  original price – discount

- **Tax:**
  To find tax, multiply the tax rate to the taxable amount (income, property value, etc.)

Example:

Original price of a microphone: $49.99, discount: 5%, tax: 5%

Selling price = 49.87

✍️ *Find the selling price of each item.*

1) Cost of a pen: $1.95, markup: 70%, discount: 40%, tax: 5%

2) Cost of a puppy: $349.99, markup: 41%, discount: 23%

3) Cost of a shirt: $14.95, markup: 25%, discount: 45%

4) Cost of an oil change: $21.95, markup: 95%

5) Cost of computer: $1,850.00, markup: 75%

Expressions and Variables

Helpful *Hints*	A variable is a letter that represents unknown numbers. A variable can be used in the same manner as all other numbers:		
	Addition	$2 + a$	2 plus a
	Subtraction	$y - 3$	y minus 3
	Division	$\dfrac{4}{x}$	4 divided by x
	Multiplication	$5a$	5 times a

✐ *Simplify each expression.*

1) $x + 5x$,

   use $x = 5$

2) $8(-3x + 9) + 6$,

   use $x = 6$

3) $10x - 2x + 6 - 5$,

   use $x = 5$

4) $2x - 3x - 9$,

   use $x = 7$

5) $(-6)(-2x - 4y)$,

   use $x = 1$, $y = 3$

6) $8x + 2 + 4y$,

   use $x = 9$, $y = 2$

7) $(-6)(-8x - 9y)$,

   use $x = 5$, $y = 5$

8) $6x + 5y$,

   use $x = 7$, $y = 4$

✐ *Simplify each expression.*

9) $5(-4 + 2x)$

10) $-3 - 5x - 6x + 9$

11) $6x - 3x - 8 + 10$

12) $(-8)(6x - 4) + 12$

13) $9(7x + 4) + 6x$

14) $(-9)(-5x + 2)$

Simplifying Variable Expressions

Helpful	– Combine "like" terms. (values with same variable and same power) **Example:**
Hints	– Use distributive property if necessary. $2x + 2\,(1 - 5x) =$
	Distributive Property: $2x + 2 - 10x = -8x + 2$
	$a\,(b + c) = ab + ac$

✎ **Simplify each expression.**

1) $-2 - x^2 - 6x^2$

2) $3 + 10x^2 + 2$

3) $8x^2 + 6x + 7x^2$

4) $5x^2 - 12x^2 + 8x$

5) $2x^2 - 2x - x$

6) $(-6)(8x - 4)$

7) $4x + 6\,(2 - 5x)$

8) $10x + 8\,(10x - 6)$

9) $9\,(-2x - 6) - 5$

10) $3\,(x + 9)$

11) $7x + 3 - 3x$

12) $2.5x^2 \times (-8x)$

✎ **Simplify.**

13) $-2(4 - 6x) - 3x$, $x = 1$

14) $2x + 8x$, $x = 2$

15) $9 - 2x + 5x + 2$, $x = 5$

16) $5\,(3x + 7)$, $x = 3$

17) $2\,(3 - 2x) - 4$, $x = 6$

18) $5x + 3x - 8$, $x = 3$

19) $x - 7x$, $x = 8$

20) $5\,(-2 - 9x)$, $x = 4$

Simplifying Polynomial Expressions

Helpful	-	In mathematics, a polynomial is an expression consisting of variables and coefficients that involves only the operations of addition, subtraction, multiplication, and non–negative integer exponents of variables.	**Example:**
Hints			An example of a polynomial of a single indeterminate x is $x^2 - 4x + 7$.
		$P(x) = a_0x^n + a_1x^{n-1} + \dots + a_{n-2}2x^2 + a_{n-1}x + a_n$	An example for three variables is $x^3 + 2xyz^2 - yz + 1$

✎**Simplify each polynomial.**

1) $4x^5 - 5x^6 + 15x^5 - 12x^6 + 3 x^6$

$19x^5 - 14x^6$

2) $(-3x^5 + 12 - 4x) + (8x^4 + 5x + 5 x^5)$

$2x^5 + x + 12 + 8x^4$

3) $10x^2 - 5x^4 + 14x^3 - 20x^4 + 15x^3 - 8x^4$

$-33x^4 + 29x^3 + 10x^2$

4) $-6x^2 + 5x^2 - 7x^3 + 12 + 22$

$-x^2 - 7x^3 + 34$

5) $12x^5 - 5x^3 + 8x^2 - 8x^5$

$4x^5 - 5x^3 + 8x^2$

6) $5x^3 + 1 + x^2 - 2x - 10x$

$5x^3 + 1 + x^2 - 12x$

7) $14x^2 - 6x^3 - 2x (4x^2 + 2x)$

$14x^2 - 6x^3 - 8x^3 - 4x^2 \rightarrow 14x^2 - 12x^3$

8) $(4x^4 - 2x) - (4x + 2x^4)$

$4x^4 - 2x - 4x + 2x^4 \rightarrow 6x^4 - 6x$

9) $(3x^2 + 1) - (4 + 2x^2)$

$3x^2 + 1 - 4 - 2x^2 \rightarrow x^2 - 3$

10) $(2x + 2) - (7x + 6)$

$2x + 2 - 7x - 6$

$-5x - 4$

11) $(12x^3 + 4x^4) - (2x^4 - 6x^3)$

$12x^3 + 4x^4 - 2x^4 + 6x^3 \rightarrow 18x^3 + 2x^4$

12) $(12 + 3x^3) + (6x^3 + 6)$

$18 + 9x^3$

13) $(5x^2 - 3) + (2x^2 - 3x^3)$

$7x^2 - 3 - 3x^3$

14) $(23x^3 - 12x^2) + (2x^2 + 9x^3)$

$32x^3 - 14x^2$

15) $(4x - 3x^3) - (3x^3 + 4x)$

$-6x^3$

Translate Phrases into an Algebraic Statement

Helpful	Translating key words and phrases into algebraic expressions:
Hints	**Addition:** plus, more than, the sum of, etc.
	Subtraction: minus, less than, decreased, etc.
	Multiplication: times, product, multiplied, etc.
	Division: quotient, divided, ratio, etc.
	Example:
	eight more than a number is 20
	$8 + x = 20$

✎ **Write an algebraic expression for each phrase.**

1) A number increased by forty–two.

2) The sum of fifteen and a number

3) The difference between fifty–six and a number.

4) The quotient of thirty and a number.

5) Twice a number decreased by 25.

6) Four times the sum of a number and -12.

7) A number divided by -20.

8) The quotient of 60 and the product of a number and -5.

9) Ten subtracted from a number.

10) The difference of six and a number.

Answers of Worksheets – Day 3

Create a Proportion

1) $1:3=2:6$

2) $12:144=1:12$

3) $2:4=8:16$

4) $5:15=9:27$

5) $7:42, 10:60$

6) $7:21=8:24$

7) $8:10=4:5$

8) $2:3=8:12$

9) $4:2=2:1$

10) $7:3=14:6$

11) $5:2=15:6$

12) $7:2=14:4$

Similar Figures

1) 5

2) 3

3) 56

Simple Interest

1) $1,690.00

2) $5,602.50

3) $37,376.00

4) $42,360.00

5) $702.00

6) $75,880.00

7) 4 years

8) $20,440

9) $500

Ratio and Rates Word Problems

1) 210

2) The ratio for both class is equal to 9 to 5.

3) Yes! Both ratios are 1 to 6

4) The price at the Quick Market is a better buy.

5) 640, the rate is 40 per hour.

6) $23.80

Percentage Calculations

1) 12.5
2) 12
3) 10.2
4) 31.5
5) 0
6) 17.6
7) 5.2
8) 42.12

9) 40
10) 2
11) 16
12) 0
13) 14
14) 33
15) 8
16) 176

17) 70
18) 72
19) 67%
20) 70%
21) 58%
22) 50%

Converting Between Percent, Fractions, and Decimals

1) 0.5
2) 0.38
3) 0.15
4) 0.8
5) 0.07
6) 0.35

7) 0.9
8) 0.2
9) 0.07
10) 50%
11) 90%
12) 0.2%

13) 52.4%
14) 10%
15) 3%
16) 363%
17) 0.8%
18) 478%

Percent Problems

1) 15
2) 104.3
3) 38.34
4) 23.44%
5) 47.6%
6) 100

7) 515.4
8) 31.98
9) 1.9%
10) 8.3 m
11) 117 inches
12) 45.7 inches

13) 49 hours
14) 62.7%
15) Mathematics
16) 600

Markup, Discount, and Tax

1) $2.09
2) $379.98
3) $10.28

4) $36.22
5) $3,237.50

Expressions and Variables

1) 30

2) −66

3) 41

4) −16

5) 84

6) 82

7) 510

8) 62

9) $10x − 20$

10) $6 − 11x$

11) $3x + 2$

12) $44 − 48x$

13) $69x + 36$

14) $45x − 18$

Simplifying Variable Expressions

1) $−7x^2 − 2$

2) $10x^2 + 5$

3) $15x^2 + 6x$

4) $−7x^2 + 8x$

5) $2x^2 − 3x$

6) $−48x + 24$

7) $−26x + 12$

8) $90x − 48$

9) $−18x − 59$

10) $3x + 27$

11) $4x + 3$

12) $−20x^3$

13) 1

14) 20

15) 26

16) 80

17) $−22$

18) 16

19) $−48$

20) $−190$

Simplifying Polynomial Expressions

1) $−14x^6 + 19x^5$

2) $2x^5 + 8x^4 + x + 12$

3) $−33x^4 + 29x^3 + 10x^2$

4) $−7x^3 − x^2 + 34$

5) $4x^5 − 5x^3 + 8x^2$

6) $5x^3 + x^2 − 12x + 1$

7) $−14x^3 + 10x^2$

8) $6x^4 − 6x$

9) $x^2 − 3$

10) $−5x − 4$

11) $2x^4 + 18x^3$

12) $9x^3 + 18$

13) $−3x^3 + 7x^2 − 3$

14) $32x^3 − 14x^2$

15) $−6x^3$

Translate Phrases into an Algebraic Statement

1) $x + 42$

2) $15 + x$

3) $56 − x$

4) $30/x$

5) $2x − 25$

6) $4(x + (−12))$

7) $\dfrac{x}{−20}$

8) $\dfrac{60}{−5x}$

9) $x − 10$

10) $6 − x$

Day 4: Equations and Inequalities

Math Topics that you'll learn today:

- ✓ The Distributive Property
- ✓ Evaluating One Variable
- ✓ Evaluating Two Variables
- ✓ Combining like Terms
- ✓ One–Step Equations
- ✓ Two–Step Equations
- ✓ Multi–Step Equations
- ✓ Graphing Single –Variable Inequalities
- ✓ One–Step Inequalities
- ✓ Two–Step Inequalities
- ✓ Multi–Step Inequalities
- ✓ Finding Slope
- ✓ Graphing Lines Using Slope–Intercept Form
- ✓ Graphing Lines Using Standard Form

Without mathematics, there's nothing you can do. Everything around you is mathematics. Everything around you is numbers." – Shakuntala Devi

The Distributive Property

Helpful	Distributive Property:	Example:
	$a\,(b\,+\,c)\,=\,ab\,+\,ac$	$3\,(4\,+\,3x)$
Hints		$=\,12\,+\,9x$

✍ **Use the distributive property to simply each expression.**

1) $-(-2-5x)$
$+2+5x \to \boxed{2+5x}$

2) $(-6x+2)(-1)$
$\boxed{6x-2}$

3) $(-5)\,(x-2)$
$\boxed{-5x+10}$

4) $-(7-3x)$
$\boxed{-7+3x}$

5) $8\,(8+2x)$
$\boxed{64+16x}$

6) $2\,(12+2x)$
$\boxed{14+4x}$

7) $(-6x+8)\,4$
$\boxed{-24x+32}$

8) $(3-6x)(-7)$
$\boxed{-21+42x}$

9) $(-12)\,(2x+1)$
$\boxed{-24x-12}$

10) $(8-2x)\,9$
$8\,\boxed{72-18x}$

11) $(-2x)(-1+9x)-4x\,(4+5x)$
$2x-18x-16x-20x^2 \to \boxed{-32x-20x^2}$

12) $3\,(-5x-3)+4(6-3x)$
$-15x-9+24+12x \to \boxed{-27x+15}$

13) $(-2)(x+4)-(2+3x)$
$-2x-8-2-3x \to \boxed{-5x-10}$

14) $(-4)(3x-2)+6\,(x+1)$
$-12x+8+6x+6 \to \boxed{-6x+14}$

15) $(-5)(4x-1)+4\,(x+2)$
$-20x+5+4x+8 \to \boxed{-16x+13}$

16) $(-3)(x+4)-(2+3x)$
$-3x-12-2+3x \;/\; \boxed{-6x-14}$

Evaluating One Variable

Helpful Hints	– To evaluate one variable expression, find the variable and substitute a number for that variable. – Perform the arithmetic operations.	**Example:** $4x + 8, x = 6$ $4(6) + 8 = 24 + 8 = 32$

✎ *Simplify each algebraic expression.*

1) $9 - x$, $x = 3$

2) $x + 2, x = 5$

3) $3x + 7, x = 6$

4) $x + (-5), x = -2$

5) $3x + 6, x = 4$

6) $4x + 6, x = -1$

7) $10 + 2x - 6, x = 3$

8) $10 - 3x, x = 8$

15) $8(5x - 12), x = -2$

9) $\dfrac{20}{x} - 3, x = 5$

10) $(-3) + \dfrac{x}{4} + 2x, x = 16$

11) $(-2) + \dfrac{x}{7}, x = 21$

12) $(-\dfrac{14}{x}) - 9 + 4x, x = 2$

13) $(-\dfrac{6}{x}) - 9 + 2x, x = 3$

14) $(-2) + \dfrac{x}{8}, x = 16$

Evaluating Two Variables

Helpful Hints	To evaluate an algebraic expression, substitute a number for each variable and perform the arithmetic operations.	**Example:**
		$2x + 4y - 3 + 2,$
		$x = 5, y = 3$
		$2(5) + 4(3) - 3 + 2$
		$= 10$
		$+ 12 - 3 + 2$
		$= 21$

✎**Simplify each algebraic expression.**

1) $2x + 4y - 3 + 2,$

   $x = 5, y = 3$

2) $(-\dfrac{12}{x}) + 1 + 5y,$

   $x = 6, y = 8$

3) $(-4)(-2a - 2b),$

   $a = 5, b = 3$

4) $10 + 3x + 7 - 2y,$

   $x = 7, y = 6$

5) $9x + 2 - 4y,$

   $x = 7, y = 5$

6) $6 + 3(-2x - 3y),$

   $x = 9, y = 7$

7) $12x + y,$

   $x = 4, y = 8$

8) $x \times 4 \div y,$

   $x = 3, y = 2$

9) $2x + 14 + 4y,$

   $x = 6, y = 8$

10) $4a - (5 - b),$

    $a = 4, b = 6$

Combining like Terms

Helpful *Hints*	– Terms are separated by "+" and "−" signs. – Like terms are terms with same variables and same powers. – Be sure to use the "+" or "−" that is in front of the coefficient.	**Example:** $22x + 6 + 2x =$ $24x + 6$

✎*Simplify each expression.*

1) $5 + 2x - 8$

2) $(-2x + 6)\,2$

3) $7 + 3x + 6x - 4$

4) $(-4) - (3)(5x + 8)$

5) $9x - 7x - 5$

6) $x - 12x$

7) $7(3x + 6) + 2x$

8) $(-11x) - 10x$

9) $3x - 12 - 5x$

10) $13 + 4x - 5$

11) $(-22x) + 8x$

12) $2(4 + 3x) - 7x$

13) $(-4x) - (6 - 14x)$

14) $5(6x - 1) + 12x$

15) $22x + 6 + 2x$

16) $(-13x) - 14x$

17) $(-6x) - 9 + 15x$

18) $(-6x) + 7x$

19) $(-5x) + 12 + 7x$

20) $(-3x) - 9 + 15x$

21) $20x - 19x$

One–Step Equations

Helpful	-	The values of two expressions on both sides of an equation are equal.	**Example:**
		$$ax + b = c$$	$-8x = 16$
Hints	-	You only need to perform one Math operation in order to solve the equation.	$x = -2$

✎ *Solve each equation.*

1) $x + 3 = 17$

2) $22 = (-8) + x$

3) $3x = (-30)$

4) $(-36) = (-6x)$

5) $(-6) = 4 + x$

6) $2 + x = (-2)$

7) $20x = (-220)$

8) $18 = x + 5$

9) $(-23) + x = (-19)$

10) $5x = (-45)$

11) $x - 12 = (-25)$

12) $x - 3 = (-12)$

13) $(-35) = x - 27$

14) $8 = 2x$

15) $(-6x) = 36$

16) $(-55) = (-5x)$

17) $x - 30 = 20$

18) $8x = 32$

19) $36 = (-4x)$

20) $4x = 68$

21) $30x = 300$

Two–Step Equations

Helpful	– You only need to perform two math operations (add, subtract, multiply, or divide) to solve the equation.	**Example:**
Hints	– Simplify using the inverse of addition or subtraction.	$-2(x-1)=42$
		$(x-1)=-21$
	– Simplify further by using the inverse of multiplication or division.	$x=-20$

✎ **Solve each equation.**

1) $5(8+x)=20$

$40+5x=20 \quad 5x=-20 \quad \boxed{x=-4}$

2) $(-7)(x-9)=42$

$-7x+63=42 \quad -7x=-21 \quad \boxed{x=3}$

3) $(-12)(2x-3)=(-12)$

$-24x+36=-12 \quad -24x=-48 \quad \boxed{x=2}$

4) $6(1+x)=12$

$6+6x=12 \quad 6x=6 \quad \boxed{x=1}$

5) $12(2x+4)=60$

$24x+48=60 \quad 24x=12 \quad \boxed{x=\tfrac{1}{2}}$

6) $7(3x+2)=42$

7) $8(14+2x)=(-34)$

8) $(-15)(2x-4)=48$

9) $3(x+5)=12$

10) $\dfrac{3x-12}{6}=4$

11) $(-12)=\dfrac{x+15}{6}$

12) $110=(-5)(2x-6)$

13) $\dfrac{x}{8}-12=4$

14) $20=12+\dfrac{x}{4}$

15) $\dfrac{-24+x}{6}=(-12)$

16) $(-4)(5+2x)=(-100)$

17) $(-12x)+20=32$

18) $\dfrac{-2+6x}{4}=(-8)$

19) $\dfrac{x+6}{5}=(-5)$

20) $(-9)+\dfrac{x}{4}=(-15)$

Multi–Step Equations

Helpful Hints	– Combine "like" terms on one side. – Bring variables to one side by adding or subtracting. – Simplify using the inverse of addition or subtraction. – Simplify further by using the inverse of multiplication or division.	**Example:** $3x + 15 = -2x + 5$ Add 2x both sides $5x + 15 = +5$ Subtract 15 both sides $5x = -10$ Divide by 5 both sides $x = -2$

✎ *Solve each equation.*

1) $-(2 - 2x) = 10$

$-2 + 2x = 10 \qquad 2x = 12$
$+2 \qquad +2 \qquad \frac{2x}{2} = \frac{12}{2} \quad \boxed{x = 6}$

2) $-12 = -(2x + 8)$

$-12 = -2x - 8 \qquad -4 = \frac{-2x}{-2} \quad \boxed{x = 2}$
$+8 \qquad +8$

3) $3x + 15 = (-2x) + 5$

$3x + 15 = -2x + 5$
$-3x \quad -3 \quad -3x \qquad 10 = -5x$
$\qquad\qquad\qquad\qquad \frac{}{-5} \quad \frac{-5x}{-5}$
$\qquad\qquad\qquad \boxed{x = -2}$

4) $-28 = (-2x) - 12x$

$-28 = -2x - 12x$
$-28 = -14x \quad \boxed{x = 2}$

5) $2(1 + 2x) + 2x = -118$

$\quad 2 + 2x + 2x = -118 \qquad \frac{4x}{4} = \frac{-120}{4}$
$\quad -2 \qquad\qquad -2$
$\qquad\qquad\qquad\qquad\qquad \boxed{x = -30}$

6) $3x - 18 = 22 + x - 3 + x$

7) $12 - 2x = (-32) - x + x$

8) $7 - 3x - 3x = 3 - 3x$

9) $6 + 10x + 3x = (-30) + 4x$

10) $(-3x) - 8(-1 + 5x) = 352$

11) $24 = (-4x) - 8 + 8$

12) $9 = 2x - 7 + 6x$

13) $6(1 + 6x) = 294$

14) $-10 = (-4x) - 6x$

15) $4x - 2 = (-7) + 5x$

16) $5x - 14 = 8x + 4$

17) $40 = -(4x - 8)$

18) $(-18) - 6x = 6(1 + 3x)$

19) $x - 5 = -2(6 + 3x)$

20) $6 = 1 - 2x + 5$

Graphing Single–Variable Inequalities

Helpful	– Isolate the variable.
	– Find the value of the inequality on the number line.
Hints	– For less than or greater than draw open circle on the value of the variable.
	– If there is an equal sign too, then use filled circle.
	– Draw a line to the right direction.

✎ **Draw a graph for each inequality.**

1) $-2 > x$

2) $\underline{5 \leq -x}$
   $\overline{-1}\overline{-1}$
   $-5 \geq x$

3) $x > 7$

4) $-x > 1.5$
   $\overline{-1}\overline{-1}$
   $x < -1.5$

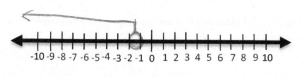

One–Step Inequalities

Helpful	– Isolate the variable.	Example:
	– For dividing both sides by negative numbers, flip the direction of the inequality sign.	$x + 4 \geq 11$
Hints		$x \geq 7$

✎**Solve each inequality and graph it.**

1) $x + 9 \geq 11$
    $-9 \quad -9$
    $x \geq 2$

2) $x - 4 \leq 2$
    $+4 \quad +4$
    $x \leq 6$

3) $\dfrac{6x}{6} \geq \dfrac{36}{6}$
    $x \geq 6$

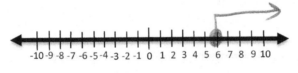

4) $7 + x < 16$
    $-7 \qquad -7$
    $x < +9$

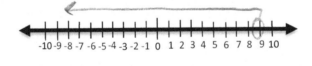

5) $x + 8 \leq 1$
    $-8 \quad -8$
    $x \leq -7$

6) $3x > 12$

7) $3x < 24$

Two–Step Inequalities

Helpful *Hints*	– Isolate the variable. – For dividing both sides by negative numbers, flip the direction of the of the inequality sign. – Simplify using the inverse of addition or subtraction. – Simplify further by using the inverse of multiplication or division.	**Example:** $2x + 9 \geq 11$ $2x \geq 2$ $x \geq 1$

✍ **Solve each inequality and graph it.**

1) $3x - 4 \leq 5$
   $+4 +4$
   $\underline{3x \leq 9}\boxed{x \leq 3}$
   33

2) $2x - 2 \leq 6$
   $+2+2$
   $\boxed{x \leq 4}$

3) $4x - 4 \leq 8$
   $+4+4$
   $\underline{4x \leq 12}\boxed{x \leq 3}$
   4

4) $3x + 6 \geq 12$
   $-6-6$
   $\underline{3x \geq 6}\boxed{x \geq 2}$
   33

5) $6x - 5 \geq 19$
   $+5+5$
   $\underline{6x \geq 24}\boxed{x \geq 4}$
   66

6) $2x - 4 \leq 6$

7) $8x - 4 \leq 4$

8) $6x + 4 \leq 10$

9) $5x + 4 \leq 9$

10) $7x - 4 \leq 3$

11) $4x - 19 < 19$

12) $2x - 3 < 21$

13) $7 + 4x \geq 19$

14) $9 + 4x < 21$

15) $3 + 2x \geq 19$

16) $6 + 4x < 22$

Multi–Step Inequalities

Helpful **Hints**	– Isolate the variable.	**Example:**
	– Simplify using the inverse of addition or subtraction.	$\dfrac{7x+1}{3} \geq 5$
	– Simplify further by using the inverse of multiplication or division.	$7x + 1 \geq 15$ $7x \geq 14$ $x \geq 7$

✎ **Solve each inequality.**

1) $\dfrac{9x}{7} - 7 < 2$

$\quad \dfrac{9x}{7} < 9 \qquad 9x - 17 < 14 \qquad \dfrac{9x}{9} < \dfrac{21}{9} \qquad \boxed{x < \dfrac{21}{9}}$
$\qquad\qquad\qquad\qquad +17 \ +17$

2) $\dfrac{4x+8}{2} \leq 12$

$\quad 4x + 8 \leq 24 \qquad \dfrac{4x}{4} \leq \dfrac{16}{4} \qquad \boxed{x \leq 4}$
$\qquad -8 \ -8$

3) $\dfrac{3x-8}{7} > 1$

$\quad 3x - 8 > 7 \qquad \dfrac{3x}{3} > \dfrac{15}{3} \qquad \boxed{x > 5}$
$\qquad +8 \ +8$

4) $-3(x-7) > 21$

$\quad -3x + 21 > 21 \qquad \dfrac{-3x}{-3} \lessgtr \dfrac{0}{-3} \qquad \boxed{x > 0} \; \boxed{x < 0}$
$\qquad -21 \ -21$

5) $4 + \dfrac{x}{3} \leq 7$

$\quad \dfrac{4}{-4} + x < 21 \qquad \boxed{x < 17}$
$\qquad\qquad -4$

6) $\dfrac{2x+6}{4} \leq 10$

Finding Slope

Helpful	Slope of a line:		Example:
Hints		$\dfrac{y_2 - y_1}{x_2 - x_1} = \dfrac{rise}{run}$	$(2, -10), (3, 6)$
			slope = 16

✎ **Find the slope of the line through each pair of points.**

1) $(1, 1), (3, 5)$

2) $(4, -6), (-3, -8)$

3) $(7, -12), (5, 10)$

4) $(19, 3), (20, 3)$

5) $(15, 8), (-17, 9)$

6) $(6, -12), (15, -3)$

7) $(3, 1), (7, -5)$

8) $(3, -2), (-7, 8)$

9) $(15, -3), (-9, 5)$

10) $(-4, 7), (-6, -4)$

11) $(6, -8), (-11, -7)$

12) $(-6, 13), (17, -9)$

13) $(-10, -2), (-6, -5)$

14) $(4, 5), (-4, 10)$

15) $(-3, 1), (-17, 2)$

16) $(7, 0), (-13, -11)$

17) $(17, -13), (17, 8)$

18) $(12, 2), (-7, 5)$

Graphing Lines Using Slope–Intercept Form

Helpful	**Slope–intercept form:** given the slope *m* and the y–intercept *b*, then the equation of the line is:
Hints	$y = mx + b.$

Example:

$y = 8x - 3$

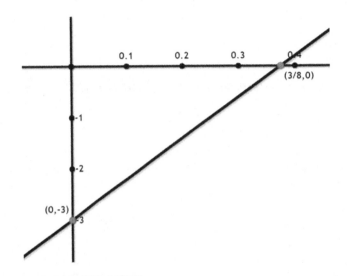

✎ **Sketch the graph of each line.**

1)

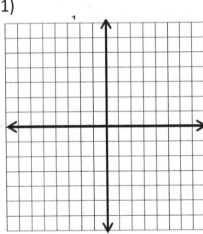

2)

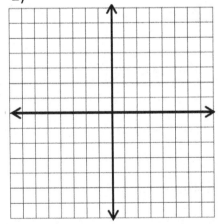

Graphing Lines Using Standard Form

<table>
<tr><td rowspan="3">*Helpful*

Hints</td><td>– Find the –intercept of the line by putting zero for y.</td></tr>
<tr><td>– Find the y–intercept of the line by putting zero for the x.</td></tr>
<tr><td>– Connect these two points.</td></tr>
</table>

Example:

$x + 4y = 12$

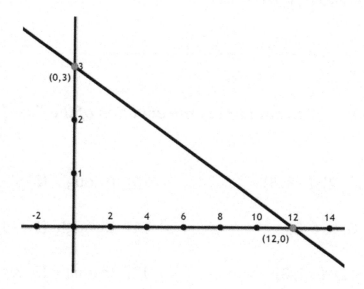

(0,3)

(12,0)

Sketch the graph of each line.

1)

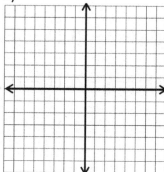

2)

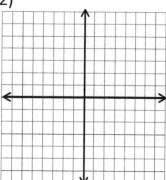

Writing Linear Equations

Helpful	The equation of a line:	**Example:**
Hints	$y = mx + b$ 1– Identify the slope. 2– Find the y–intercept. This can be done by substituting the slope and the coordinates of a point (x, y) on the line.	through: $(-4, -2), (-3, 5)$ $y = 7x + 26$

✍ *Write the slope–intercept form of the equation of the line through the given points.*

1) through: $(-4, -2), (-3, 5)$

2) through: $(5, 4), (-4, 3)$

3) through: $(0, -2), (-5, 3)$

4) through: $(-1, 1), (-2, 6)$

5) through: $(0, 3), (-4, -1)$

6) through: $(0, 2), (1, -3)$

7) through: $(0, -5), (4, 3)$

8) through: $(-1, 4), (0, 4)$

9) through: $(2, -3), (3, -5)$

10) through: $(2, 5), (-1, -4)$

11) through: $(1, -3), (-3, 1)$

12) through: $(3, 3), (1, -5)$

13) through: $(4, 4), (3, -5)$

14) through: $(0, 3), (1, 1)$

15) through: $(5, 5), (2, -3)$

16) through: $(-2, -2), (2, -5)$

17) through: $(-3, -2), (1, -1)$

18) through: $(1, 5), (4, 1)$

Graphing Linear Inequalities

Helpful	1– First, graph the "equals" line.
	2– Choose a testing point. (it can be any point on both sides of the line.)
Hints	3– Put the value of (x, y) of that point in the inequality. If that works, that part of the line is the solution. If the values don't work, then the other part of the line is the solution.

Sketch the graph of each linear inequality.

1)

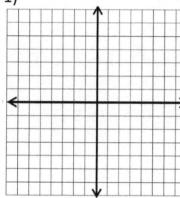

2)

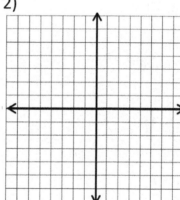

4)

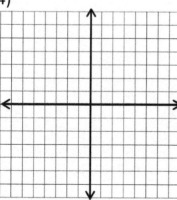

5)

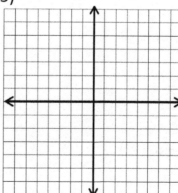

Finding Midpoint

Helpful	Midpoint of the segment AB:	Example:
		(3, 9), (− 1, 6)
Hints	$M\left(\dfrac{x_1+x_2}{2}, \dfrac{y_1+y_2}{2}\right)$	M (1, 7.5)

✎ **Find the midpoint of the line segment with the given endpoints.**

1) (2, − 2), (3, − 5)

  $M\left(\dfrac{5}{2}, \dfrac{-7}{2}\right)$

2) (0, 2), (− 2, − 6)

  $M(−1, −2)$

3) (7, 4), (9, − 1)

  $M\left(\dfrac{16}{2}, \dfrac{3}{2}\right) = M\left(8, \dfrac{3}{2}\right)$

4) (4, − 5), (0, 8)

5) (1, − 2), (1, − 6)

6) (− 2, − 3), (3, − 6)

7) (7, 0), (− 7, 5)

8) (− 2, 6), (− 3, − 2)

9) (− 1, 1), (5, − 5)

10) (2.3, − 1.3), (− 2.2, − 0.5)

11) (4.1, 6.32), (4, 5.6)

12) (2, − 1), (− 6, 0)

13) (− 4, 4), (5, − 1)

14) (− 2, − 3), (− 6, 5)

15) ($\frac{1}{2}$, 1), (2, 4)

16) (− 2, − 2), (6, 5)

Finding Distance of Two Points

Helpful	Distance from A to B:	**Example:**
Hints	$d = \sqrt{(x_1 - x_2)^2 + (y_1 - y_2)^2}$	$(-1, 2), (-1, -7)$
		Distance = 9

✎ **Find the distance between each pair of points.**

1) $(2, -1), (1, -1)$
     $-1 + 1 = 0$
     $d = \sqrt{1}$
     $2 - 1 = 1^2 =$ $d\sqrt{1 + 0}$ 1

2) $(6, 4), (-1, 3)$

3) $(-8, -5), (-6, 1)$
   $d = \sqrt{64+1}$ $49 + 1 d = \sqrt{50}$ $5\sqrt{2}$
   $d = \sqrt{40}$ $d = \sqrt{(8+6)^2 4 + -6^2}$ 10 5
   $20 \quad 2$ $(\pm 2) \quad -36$ $5 \quad 2$ $5\sqrt{2}$
   $5 \quad 4$

4) $(-6, -10), (-2, -10)$ $2\sqrt{10}$
   $2 \quad 2$
   $d\sqrt{16 +}$ $\boxed{4}$

5) $(4, -6), (-3, 4)$

6) $(-6, -7), (-2, -8)$

7) $(5, 4), (8, 2)$

8) $(8, 4), (3, -7)$

9) $(1, 3), (5, 7)$

10) $(4, 2), (-7, 1)$

11) $(-3, -4), (-7, -2)$

12) $(-7, -2), (6, 9)$

13) $(10, 0), (0, 4)$

14) $(-3, 2), (5, 0)$

15) $(-5, 6), (8, -4)$

16) $(3, -5), (-8, -4)$

17) $(0, 8), (4, 10)$

18) $(6, 4), (-5, -1)$

Answers of Worksheets – Day 4

The Distributive Property

1) 5x + 2
2) 6x − 2
3) −5x + 10
4) 3x − 7
5) 16x + 64
6) 4x + 24

7) − 24x + 32
8) 42x − 21
9) − 24x − 12
10) − 18x + 72
11) − 38x^2 − 14x
12) − 27x + 15

13) − 5x − 10
14) − 6x + 14
15) − 16x + 13
16) − 6x − 14

Evaluating One Variable

1) 6
2) 7
3) 25
4) −7
5) 18

6) 2
7) 10
8) −14
9) 1
10) 33

11) 1
12) −8
13) −5
14) 0
15) −176

Evaluating Two Variables

1) 21
2) 39
3) 64
4) 26

5) 45
6) −111
7) 56
8) 6

9) 58
10) 17

Combining like Terms

1) 2x − 3
2) −4x + 12
3) 9x + 3
4) −15x − 28
5) 2x − 5
6) −11x
7) 23x + 42

8) −21x
9) −2x − 12
10) 4x + 8
11) −14x
12) − x + 8
13) 10x − 6
14) 42x − 5

15) 24x + 6
16) −27x
17) 9x − 9
18) x
19) 2x + 12
20) 12x − 9
21) x

One–Step Equations

1) 14	9) 4	17) 50
2) 30	10) − 9	18) 4
3) − 10	11) − 13	19) − 9
4) 6	12) − 9	20) 17
5) − 10	13) − 8	21) 10
6) − 4	14) 4	
7) − 11	15) − 6	
8) 13	16) 11	

Two–Step Equations

1) − 4	8) $\frac{2}{5}$	15) − 48
2) 3	9) − 1	16) 10
3) 2	10) 12	17) − 1
4) 1	11) − 87	18) − 5
5) 0.5	12) − 8	19) − 31
6) $\frac{4}{3}$	13) 128	20) − 24
7) $-\frac{73}{8}$	14) 32	

Multi–Step Equations

1) 6	8) $\frac{4}{3}$	14) 1
2) 2	9) − 4	15) 5
3) − 2	10) − 8	16) − 6
4) 2	11) − 6	17) − 8
5) − 20	12) 2	18) − 1
6) 37	13) 8	19) − 1
7) 22		20) 0

Graphing Single–Variable Inequalities

1) $-2 > x$

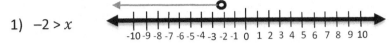

2) $x \leq -5$

3) $x > 7$

4) $-1.5 > x$

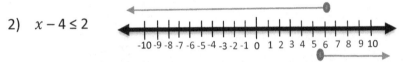

One–Step Inequalities

1) $x + 9 \geq 11$

2) $x - 4 \leq 2$

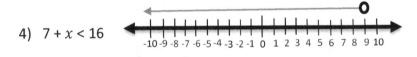

3) $6x \geq 36$

4) $7 + x < 16$

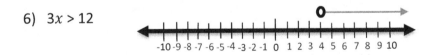

5) $x + 8 \leq 1$

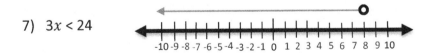

6) $3x > 12$

7) $3x < 24$

Two–Step inequalities

1) $x \leq 3$

2) $x \leq 4$

3) $x \leq 3$

4) $x \geq 2$

5) $x \geq 4$

6) $x \leq 5$

7) $x \leq 1$

8) $x \leq 1$

9) $x \leq 1$

10) $x \leq 1$

11) $x < 9.5$

12) $x < 12$

13) $x \geq 3$

14) $x < 3$

15) $x \geq 8$

16) $x < 4$

Multi–Step inequalities

1) $x < 7$

2) $x \leq 4$

3) $x > 5$

4) $x < 0$

5) $x < 9$

6) $x \leq 17$

Finding Slope

1) 2

2) $\dfrac{2}{7}$

3) -11

4) 0

5) $-\dfrac{1}{32}$

6) 1

7) $-\dfrac{3}{2}$

8) -1

9) $-\dfrac{1}{3}$

10) $\dfrac{11}{2}$

11) $-\dfrac{1}{17}$

12) $-\dfrac{22}{23}$

13) $-\dfrac{3}{4}$

14) $-\dfrac{5}{8}$

15) $-\dfrac{1}{14}$

16) $\dfrac{11}{20}$

17) Undefined

18) $-\dfrac{3}{19}$

Graphing Lines Using Slope–Intercept Form

1)

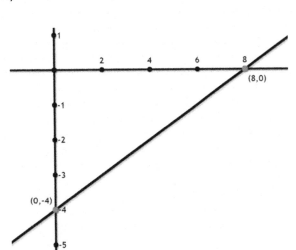

2)

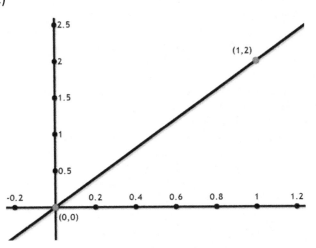

Graphing Lines Using Standard Form

1)

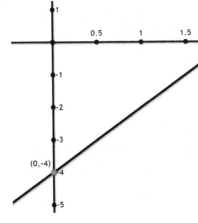

2)

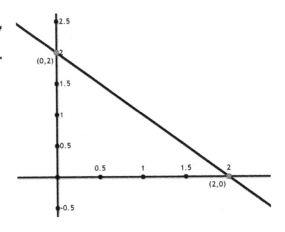

Writing Linear Equations

1) $y = 7x + 26$

2) $y = \frac{1}{9}x + \frac{31}{9}$

3) $y = -x - 2$

4) $y = -5x - 4$

5) $y = x + 3$

6) $y = -5x + 2$

7) $y = 2x - 5$

8) $y = 4$

9) $y = -2x + 1$

10) $y = 3x - 1$

11) $y = -x - 2$

12) $y = 4x - 9$

13) $y = 9x - 32$

14) $y = -2x + 3$

15) $y = \frac{8}{3}x - \frac{25}{3}$

16) $y = -\frac{3}{4}x - \frac{7}{2}$

17) $y = \frac{1}{4}x - \frac{5}{4}$

18) $y = -\frac{4}{3}x + \frac{19}{3}$

Graphing Linear Inequalities

1)

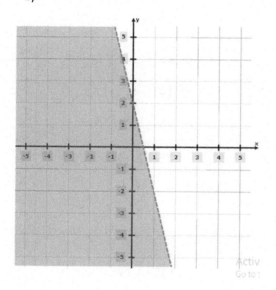

2)

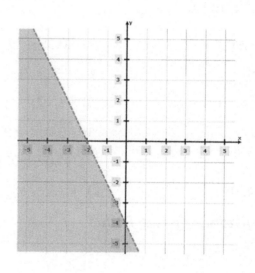

4)

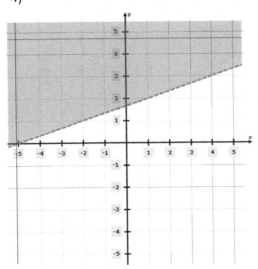

5)

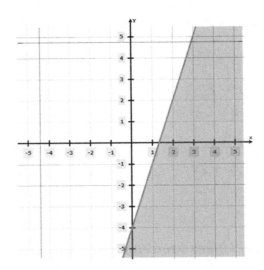

Finding Midpoint

1) (2.5, −3.5)

2) (−1, −2)

3) (8, 1.5)

4) (2, 1.5)

5) (1, −4)

6) (0.5, −4.5)

7) (0, 2.5)

8) (−2.5, 2)

9) (2, −2)

10) (0.05, −0.9)

11) (4.05, 5.96)

12) (−2, − 0.5)

13) $(\frac{1}{2}, 1\frac{1}{2})$

14) (−4, 1)

15) (1.25, 2.5)

16) $(2, \frac{3}{2})$

Finding Distance of Two Points

1) 1

2) 7.1

3) 6.32

4) 4

5) 12.21

6) 4.12

7) 3.61

8) 12.1

9) 5.66

10) 11.04

11) 4.47

12) 17.03

13) 10.77

14) 8.25

15) 16.4

16) 10.3

17) 4.47

18) 12.1

Day 5: Monomials and Polynomials

Math Topics that you'll learn today:

- ✓ Writing Linear Equations
- ✓ Graphing Linear Inequalities
- ✓ Finding Midpoint
- ✓ Finding Distance of Two Points
- ✓ Classifying Polynomials
- ✓ Writing Polynomials in Standard Form
- ✓ Simplifying Polynomials
- ✓ Adding and Subtracting Polynomials
- ✓ Multiplying Monomials
- ✓ Multiplying and Dividing Monomials

- ✓ Multiplying a Polynomial and a Monomial
- ✓ Multiplying Binomials
- ✓ Factoring Trinomials
- ✓ Operations with Polynomials
- ✓ Solve a Quadratic Equation
- ✓ Solving Systems of Equations by Substitution
- ✓ Solving Systems of Equations by Elimination
- ✓ Systems of Equations Word Problems

Mathematics – the unshaken Foundation of Sciences, and the plentiful Fountain of Advantage to human affairs. — Isaac Barrow

Classifying Polynomials

Helpful

Hints

Name	Degree	Example
constant	0	4
linear	1	$2x$
quadratic	2	$x^2 + 5x + 6$
cubic	3	$x^3 - x^2 + 4x + 8$
quartic	4	$x^4 + 3x^3 - x^2 + 2x + 6$
quantic	5	$x^5 - 2x^4 + x^3 - x^2 + x + 10$

✎ *Name each polynomial by degree and number of terms.*

1) x

2) $-5x^4$

    4, 1

3) $7x - 4$

    1, 2

4) -6

    0, 1

5) $8x + 1$

    1, 2

6) $9x^2 - 8x^3$

7) $2x^5$

8) $10 + 8x$

9) $5x^2 - 6x$

10) $-7x^7 + 7x^4$

11) $-8x^4 + 5x^3 - 2x^2 - 8x$

12) $4x - 9x^2 + 4x^3 - 5x^4$

13) $4x^6 + 5x^5 + x^4$

14) $-4 - 2x^2 + 8x$

15) $9x^6 - 8$

16) $7x^5 + 10x^4 - 3x + 10x^7$

17) $4x^6 - 3x^2 - 8x^4$

18) $-5x^4 + 10x - 10$

Writing Polynomials in Standard Form

Helpful	A polynomial function $f(x)$ of degree n is of the form	**Example:**
Hints	$f(x) = a_n x^n + a_{n-1} x^{n-1} + \dots + a_1 x + a_0$	$2x^2 - 4x^3 - x =$
	The first term is the one with the biggest power!	$-4x^3 + 2x^2 - x$

✎ **Write each polynomial in standard form.**

1) $3x^2 - 5x^3$

$-5x^3 + 3x^2$

2) $3 + 4x^3 - 3$

$4x^3$

3) $2x^2 + 1x - 6x^3$

$-6x^3 + 2x^2 + 1x$

4) $9x - 7x$

$2x$

5) $12 - 7x + 9x^4$

$9x^4 - 7x + 12$

6) $5x^2 + 13x - 2x^3$

$-2x^3 + 5x^2 + 13x$

7) $-3 + 16x - 16x$

8) $3x(x + 4) - 2(x + 4)$

9) $(x + 5)(x - 2)$

10) $3x^2 + x + 12 - 5x^2 - 2x$

11) $12x^5 + 7x^3 - 3x^5 - 8x^3$

12) $3x(2x + 5 - 2x^2)$

13) $11x(x^5 + 2x^3)$

14) $(x + 6)(x + 3)$

15) $(x + 4)^2$

16) $(8x - 7)(3x + 2)$

17) $5x(3x^2 + 2x + 1)$

18) $7x(3 - x + 6x^3)$

Simplifying Polynomials

Helpful	1– Find "like" terms. (they have same variables with same power).	Example:
Hints	2– Add or Subtract "like" terms using PEMDAS operation.	$2x^5 - 3x^3 + 8x^2 - 2x^5 =$ $- 3x^3 + 8x^2$

✎ Simplify each expression.

1) $11 - 4x^2 + 3x^2 - 7x^3 + 3$

$-7x^3 - x^2 + 14$

2) $2x^5 - x^3 + 8x^2 - 2x^5$

$-2x^5 - x^3 + -x^3 + 8x^2$

3) $(-5)(x^6 + 10) - 8(14 - x^6)$

$-50 + 5x^6 - 112 + 8x^6$
$-162 + 13x^6 \quad 3x^6 - 162$

4) $4(2x^2 + 4x^2 - 3x^3) + 6x^3 + 17$

5) $11 - 6x^2 + 5x^2 - 12x^3 + 22$

6) $2x^2 - 2x + 3x^3 + 12x - 22x$

7) $(3x - 8)(3x - 4)$

8) $(12x + 2y)^2$

9) $(12x^3 + 28x^2 + 10x + 4) \div (x + 2)$

10) $(2x + 12x^2 - 2) \div (2x + 1)$

11) $(2x^3 - 1) + (3x^3 - 2x^3)$

12) $(x - 5)(x - 3)$

13) $(3x + 8)(3x - 8)$

14) $(8x^2 - 3x) - (5x - 5 - 8x^2)$

Adding and Subtracting Polynomials

Helpful	Adding polynomials is just a matter of combining like terms, with some order of operations considerations thrown in.	Example:
Hints	Be careful with the minus signs, and don't confuse addition and multiplication!	$(3x^3 - 1) - (4x^3 + 2)$ $= -x^3 - 3$

✎**Simplify each expression.**

1) $(2x^3 - 2) + (2x^3 + 2)$

$2x^3 - 2 + 2x^3 + 2$ $\boxed{4x^3}$

2) $(4x^3 + 5) - (7 - 2x^3)$

$4x^3 + 5 - 7 + 2x^3$ $\boxed{6x^3 - 2}$

3) $(4x^2 + 2x^3) - (2x^3 + 5)$

$4x^2 + 2x^3 - 2x^3 - 5$ $\boxed{4x^2 - 5}$

4) $(4x^2 - x) + (3x - 5x^2)$

5) $(7x + 9) - (3x + 9)$

6) $(4x^4 - 2x) - (6x - 2x^4)$

7) $(12x - 4x^3) - (8x^3 + 6x)$

8) $(2x^3 - 8x^2) - (5x^2 - 3x^3)$

9) $(2x^2 - 6) + (9x^2 - 4x^3)$

10) $(4x^3 + 3x^4) - (x^4 - 5x^3)$

11) $(-12x^4 + 10x^5 + 2x^3) + (14x^3 + 23x^5 + 8x^4)$

12) $(13x^2 - 6x^5 - 2x) - (-10x^2 - 11x^5 + 9x)$

13) $(35 + 9x^5 - 3x^2) + (8x^4 + 3x^5) - (27 - 5x^4)$

14) $(3x^5 - 2x^3 - 4x) + (4x + 10x^4 - 23) + (x^2 - x^3 + 12)$

Multiplying Monomials

Helpful	A monomial is a polynomial with just one term, like $2x$ or $7y$.	**Example:**
Hints		$2u^3 \times (-3u)$ $= -6u^4$

✎ *Simplify each expression.*

1) $2xy^2z \times 4z^2$

$2xy^2 \times 4z^3 =$

$8xyz^3$

2) $4xy \times x^2y$

$4x^3y^2$

3) $4pq^3 \times (-2p^4q)$

$-8p^5q^4$

4) $8s^4t^2 \times st^5$

$8s^5t^7$

5) $12p^3 \times (-3p^4)$

$-36p^7$

6) $-4p^2q^3r \times 6pq^2r^3$

7) $(-8a^4) \times (-12a^6b)$

8) $3u^4v^2 \times (-7u^2v^3)$

9) $4u^3 \times (-2u)$

10) $-6xy^2 \times 3x^2y$

11) $12y^2z^3 \times (-y^2z)$

12) $5a^2bc^2 \times 2abc^2$

100

Multiplying and Dividing Monomials

Helpful	- When you divide two monomials you need to divide their coefficients and then divide their variables.
Hints	- In case of exponents with the same base, you need to subtract their powers.

Example:

$(-3x^2)(8x^4y^{12}) = -24x^6y^{12}$

$\dfrac{36\,x^5y^7}{4\,x^4y^5} = 9xy^2$

✎ *Simplify.*

1) $(7x^4y^6)(4x^3y^4)$

$28x^ny^{10}$

2) $(15x^4)(3x^9)$

$45x^{13}$

3) $(12x^2y^9)(7x^9y^{12})$

4) $\dfrac{80\,x^{12}y^9}{10\,x^6y^7}$

5) $\dfrac{95\,x^{18}y^7}{5\,x^9y^2}$

$19x^9y^5$

6) $\dfrac{200\,x^3y^8}{40\,x^3y^7}$

$5\text{\o}y$

7) $\dfrac{-15\,x^{17}y^{13}}{3\,x^6y^9}$

$-5x^{11}y^4$

8) $\dfrac{-64\,x^8y^{10}}{8\,x^3y^7}$

Multiplying a Polynomial and a Monomial

Helpful	– When multiplying monomials, use the product rule for exponents.	**Example:**
Hints	– When multiplying a monomial by a polynomial, use the distributive property.	$2x(8x-2) =$
	$a \times (b+c) = a \times b + a \times c$	$16x^2 - 4x$

✍ **Find each product.**

1) $5(3x-6y)$

$15x-30y$

2) $9x(2x+4y)$

$18x^2 + 36xy$

3) $8x(7x-4)$

$56x^2 - 32x$

4) $12x(3x+9)$

$36x^2 + 108x$

5) $11x(2x-11y)$

$22x^2 - 121xy$

6) $2x(6x-6y)$

7) $3x(2x^2-3x+8)$

8) $13x(4x+8y)$

9) $20(2x^2-8x-5)$

10) $3x(3x-2)$

11) $6x^3(3x^2-2x+2)$

12) $8x^2(3x^2-5xy+7y^2)$

13) $2x^2(3x^2-5x+12)$

14) $2x^3(2x^2+5x-4)$

15) $5x(6x^2-5xy+2y^2)$

$30x^3 - 25x^2y + 10xy^2$

16) $9(x^2+xy-8y^2)$

Multiplying Binomials

Helpful *Hints*	Use "FOIL". (First–Out–In–Last) $(x + a)(x + b) = x^2 + (b + a)x + ab$	**Example:** $(x + 2)(x - 3) =$ $x^2 - x - 6$

✎**Multiply.**

1) $(3x - 2)(4x + 2)$

$12x^2 + 6x - 8x - 4$

$\boxed{12x^2 - 2x - 4}$

2) $(2x - 5)(x + 7)$

$2x^2 + 14x - 5x - 35$

3) $(x + 2)(x + 8)$ $\boxed{2x^2 + 9x - 35}$

4) $(x^2 + 2)(x^2 - 2)$

5) $(x - 2)(x + 4)$

6) $(x - 8)(2x + 8)$

7) $(5x - 4)(3x + 3)$

8) $(x - 7)(x - 6)$

9) $(6x + 9)(4x + 9)$

10) $(2x - 6)(5x + 6)$

11) $(x - 7)(x + 7)$

12) $(x + 4)(4x - 8)$

13) $(6x - 4)(6x + 4)$

14) $(x - 7)(x + 2)$

15) $(x - 8)(x + 8)$

16) $(3x + 3)(3x - 4)$

17) $(x + 3)(x + 3)$

18) $(x + 4)(x + 6)$

Factoring Trinomials

Helpful	"FOIL"	Example:
	$(x + a)(x + b) = x^2 + (b + a)x + ab$	$x^2 + 5x + 6 =$
Hints	"Difference of Squares"	$(x + 2)(x + 3)$
	$a^2 - b^2 = (a + b)(a - b)$	
	$a^2 + 2ab + b^2 = (a + b)(a + b)$	
	$a^2 - 2ab + b^2 = (a - b)(a - b)$	
	"Reverse FOIL"	
	$x^2 + (b + a)x + ab = (x + a)(x + b)$	

✎ **Factor each trinomial.**

1) $x^2 - 7x + 12$

   $(x-3),(x+4)$

2) $x^2 + 5x - 14$

   $(x-2)(x+7)$

3) $x^2 - 11x - 42$

   $(x-3)(x+14)$

4) $6x^2 + x - 12$

5) $x^2 - 17x + 30$

6) $x^2 + 8x + 15$

7) $3x^2 + 11x - 4$

8) $x^2 - 6x - 27$

9) $10x^2 + 33x - 7$

10) $x^2 + 24x + 144$

11) $49x^2 + 28xy + 4y^2$

12) $16x^2 - 40x + 25$

13) $x^2 - 10x + 25$

14) $25x^2 - 20x + 4$

15) $x^3 + 6x^2y^2 + 9xy^3$

16) $9x^2 + 24x + 16$

17) $x^2 - 8x + 16$

18) $x^2 + 121 + 22x$

Operations with Polynomials

Helpful	– When multiplying a monomial by a polynomial, use the distributive property.	**Example:**
Hints	a × (b + c) = a × b + a × c	5 (6x – 1) =
		30x – 5

✎ **Find each product.**

1) $3x^2 (6x - 5)$

$18x^3 - 15x$

2) $5x^2 (7x - 2)$

$35x^3 - 10x^2$

3) $-3 (8x - 3)$

$-24x + 9$

4) $6x^3 (-3x + 4)$

$-18x^4 + 24x^3$

5) $9 (6x + 2)$

6) $8 (3x + 7)$

7) $5 (6x - 1)$

8) $-7x^4 (2x - 4)$

9) $8 (x^2 + 2x - 3)$

10) $4 (4x^2 - 2x + 1)$

11) $2 (3x^2 + 2x - 2)$

12) $8x (5x^2 + 3x + 8)$

13) $(9x + 1) (3x - 1)$

14) $(4x + 5) (6x - 5)$

15) $(7x + 3) (5x - 6)$

16) $(3x - 4) (3x + 8)$

Solve a Quadratic Equation

| **Helpful**

Hints | Write the equation in the form of $ax^2 + bx + c = 0$

Factorize the quadratic.

Use quadratic formula if you couldn't factorize the quadratic.

Quadratic formula

$$x = \frac{-b \pm \sqrt{b^2 - 4ac}}{2a}$$ | **Example:**

$x^2 + 5x + 6 = 0$

$(x + 3)(x + 2) = 0$

$(x + 3) = 0$

$x = -3$

$x + 2 = 0$

$x = -2$ |

(handwritten margin work) $-45 \pm \sqrt{45^2 - 4 \times 18 \times (-20)}$ ... 2×18

📝Solve each equation.

(handwritten margin work) $x^2 - 10x + 24 = 0$; $(x \quad -12)(x \quad +2)$; $(x-12)(x+2)=0$; $x = -2 \text{ or } 12$

1) $(x + 2)(x - 4) = 0$

(handwritten) $x = -2$, $x = -4$

2) $(x + 5)(x + 8) = 0$

(handwritten) $x = -5$, $x = -8$

3) $(3x + 2)(x + 3) = 0$

4) $(4x + 7)(2x + 5) = 0$

5) $x^2 - 11x + 19 = -5$

6) $x^2 + 7x + 18 = 8$

7) $x^2 - 10x + 22 = -2$

8) $x^2 + 3x - 12 = 6$

9) $18x^2 + 45x - 27 = 0$

10) $90x^2 - 84x = -18$

11) $x^2 + 8x = -15$

(handwritten) 3×8

(handwritten) $18x^2 + 45x - 27 = 0$; $a \quad b \quad c$; 3

(handwritten) $a = 18$; $b = 45$; $c = -27$

Solving Systems of Equations by Substitution

Helpful Hints	Consider the system of equations x – y = 1, –2x + y = 6 Substitute x = 1 – y in the second equation -2(1-y) + y = 5 y = 2 Substitute y = 2 in x = 1 + y X = 1 + 2 = 3	**Example:** – 2x – 2y = -13 – 4x + 2y = 10 (0.5, 6)

✎Solve each system of equation by substitution.

x·y

1) $– 2x + 2y = 4$

$– 2x + y = 3$ $-2x +2y= 4$
                  $-2x + y = \cancel{0}3$
        $y=1$

2) $– 10x + 2y = – 6$ $-2x+2y= 4$

$6x – 16y = 48$ $2x - y = -3$
                  $y = 1$

3) $y = – 8$

$16x – 12y = 72$

4) $2y = – 6x + 10$

$10x – 8y = – 6$

5) $3x – 9y = – 3$

$3y = 3x – 3$

6) $– 4x + 12y = 12$

$– 14x + 16y = – 10$

$18x^2 +45x - 2\eta = 0$
$2x$ $+ 3$
Px $+ 9$ $x2$ $\dfrac{2\eta x}{18 x}$

Solving Systems of Equations by Elimination

Helpful	-	The elimination method for solving systems of linear equations uses the addition property of equality. You can add the same value to each side of an equation.	**Example:**
Hints			$x + 2y = 6$ $+ -x + y = 3$

$$3y = 9$$

$$y = 3$$

$$x + 6 = 6$$

$$x = 0$$

✍ **Solve each system of equation by elimination.**

1) $10x - 9y = -12$

    $- 5x + 3y = 6$

2) $- 3x - 4y = 5$

    $x - 2y = 5$

3) $5x - 14y = 22$

    $- 6x + 7y = 3$

4) $10x - 14y = -4$

    $- 10x - 20y = -30$

5) $32x + 14y = 52$

    $16x - 4y = -40$

6) $2x - 8y = -6$

    $8x + 2y = 10$

7) $- 4x + 4y = -4$

    $4x + 2y = 10$

8) $4x + 6y = 10$

    $8x + 12y = -20$

Systems of Equations Word Problems

Helpful	Define your variables, Write two equations, and Use one of the methods for solving systems of equations to solve.
Hints	

Example:

The difference of two numbers is 6. Their sum is 14. Find the numbers.

$x + y = 6$

$x + y = 14$ (10, 4)

[handwritten: $x - y = 6$ $x + y = 14$]

[handwritten: $x + y = 10$, $4x + 8y = 34$, $4x + 5y = 16$]

✎Solve.

1) A farmhouse shelters 10 animals, some are pigs and some are ducks. Altogether there are 36 legs. How many of each animal are there?

[handwritten: $x + y = 10 \quad 2x + y = 5 \quad 2x + y = 18$, $y = \quad x + y = 10$, $x + y = 10 \quad 3x + y = 26 \quad (x = 8, y = 2)$, $4x + 2y = 36$]

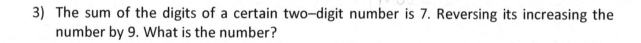

2) A class Of 195 students went on a field trip. They took vehicles, some cars and some buses. Find the number of cars and the number of buses they took if each car holds 5 students and each bus hold 45 students.

3) The sum of the digits of a certain two–digit number is 7. Reversing its increasing the number by 9. What is the number?

4) A boat traveled 336 miles downstream and back. The trip downstream took 12 hours. The trip back took 14 hours. What is the speed of the boat in still water? What is the speed of the current?

Answers of Worksheets – Day 5

Classifying Polynomials

1) Linear monomial
2) Quartic monomial
3) Linear binomial
4) Constant monomial
5) Linear binomial
11) Quartic polynomial with four terms
12) Quartic polynomial with four terms
13) Sixth degree trinomial
14) Quadratic trinomial
15) Sixth degree binomial

6) Cubic binomial
7) Quantic monomial
8) Linear binomial
9) Quadratic binomial
10) Seventh degree binomial
16) Seventh degree polynomial with four terms
17) Sixth degree trinomial
18) Quartic trinomial

Writing Polynomials in Standard Form

1) $-5x^3 + 3x^2$
2) $4x^3$
3) $-6x^3 + 2x^2 + x$
4) $2x$
5) $9x^4 - 7x + 12$
6) $-2x^3 + 5x^2 + 13x$
7) -3
8) $3x^2 + 10x - 8$
9) $x^2 + 3x - 10$

10) $-2x^2 - x + 12$
11) $9x^5 - x^3$
12) $-6x^3 + 6x^2 + 15x$
13) $11x^6 + 22x^4$
14) $x^2 + 9x + 18$
15) $x^2 + 8x + 16$
16) $24x^2 - 5x - 14$
17) $15x^3 + 10x^2 + 5x$
18) $42 - 7x^2 + 21x$

Simplifying Polynomials

1) $-7x^3 - x^2 + 14$
2) $-x^3 + 8x^2$
3) $3x^6 - 162$

4) $-6x^3 + 24x^2 + 17$
5) $-12x^3 - x^2 + 33$
6) $3x^3 + 2x^2 - 12x$

7) $9x^2 - 36x + 32$

8) $144x^2 + 48xy + 4y^2$

9) $12x^2 + 4x + 2$

10) $6x - 1$

11) $3x^3 - 1$

12) $x^2 - 8x + 15$

13) $9x^2 - 64$

14) $16x^2 - 8x + 5$

Adding and Subtracting Polynomials

1) $4x^3$

2) $6x^3 - 2$

3) $4x^2 - 5$

4) $-x^2 + 2x$

5) $4x$

6) $6x^4 - 8x$

7) $-12x^3 + 6x$

8) $5x^3 - 13x^2$

9) $-4x^3 + 11x^2 - 6$

10) $2x^4 + 9x^3$

11) $33x^5 - 4x^4 + 16x^3$

12) $5x^5 + 23x^2 - 11x$

13) $12x^5 + 13x^4 - 3x^2 + 8$

14) $3x^5 + 10x^4 - 3x^3 + x^2 - 11$

Multiplying Monomials

1) $8xy^2z^3$

2) $4x^3y^2$

3) $-8p^5q^4$

4) $8s^5t^7$

5) $-36p^7$

6) $-24p^3q^5r^4$

7) $96a^{10}b$

8) $-21u^6v^5$

9) $-8u^4$

10) $-18x^3y^3$

11) $-12y^4z^4$

12) $10a^3b^2c^4$

Multiplying and Dividing Monomials

1) $28x^7y^{10}$

2) $45x^{13}$

3) $84x^{11}y^{21}$

4) $8x^6y^2$

5) $19x^9y^5$

6) $5y$

7) $-5x^{11}y^4$

8) $-8x^5y^3$

Multiplying a Polynomial and a Monomial

1) $15x - 30y$

2) $18x^2 + 36xy$

3) $56x^2 - 32x$

4) $36x^2 + 108x$

5) $22x^2 - 121xy$

6) $12x^2 - 12xy$

7) $6x^3 - 9x^2 + 24x$

8) $52x^2 + 104xy$

9) $40x^2 - 160x - 100$

10) $9x^2 - 6x$

11) $18x^5 - 12x^4 + 12x^3$

12) $24x^4 - 40x^3y + 56y^2x^2$

13) $6x^4 - 10x^3 + 24x^2$

14) $4x^5 + 10x^4 - 8x^3$

15) $30x^3 - 25x^2y + 10xy^2$

16) $9x^2 + 9xy - 72y^2$

Multiplying Binomials

1) $12x^2 - 2x - 4$

2) $2x^2 + 9x - 35$

3) $x^2 + 10x + 16$

4) $x^4 - 4$

5) $x^2 + 2x - 8$

6) $2x^2 - 8x - 64$

7) $15x^2 + 3x - 12$

8) $x^2 - 13x + 42$

9) $24x^2 + 90x + 81$

10) $10x^2 - 18x - 36$

11) $x^2 - 49$

12) $4x^2 + 8x - 32$

13) $36x^2 - 16$

14) $x^2 - 5x - 14$

15) $x^2 - 64$

16) $9x^2 - 3x - 12$

17) $x^2 + 6x + 9$

18) $x^2 + 10x + 24$

Factoring Trinomials

1) $(x - 3)(x - 4)$

2) $(x - 2)(x + 7)$

3) $(x + 3)(x - 14)$

4) $(2x + 3)(3x - 4)$

5) $(x - 15)(x - 2)$

6) $(x + 3)(x + 5)$

7) $(3x - 1)(x + 4)$

8) $(x - 9)(x + 3)$

9) $(5x - 1)(2x + 7)$

10) $(x + 12)(x + 12)$

11) $(7x + 2y)(7x + 2y)$

12) $(4x - 5)(4x - 5)$

13) $(x - 5)(x - 5)$

14) $(5x - 2)(5x - 2)$

15) $x(x^2 + 6xy^2 + 9y^3)$

16) $(3x + 4)(3x + 4)$

17) $(x - 4)(x - 4)$

18) $(x + 11)(x + 11)$

Operations with Polynomials

1) $18x^3 - 15x^2$

2) $35x^3 - 10x^2$

3) $-24x + 9$

4) $-18x^4 + 24x^3$

5) $54x + 18$

6) $24x + 56$

7) $30x - 5$

8) $-14x^5 + 28x^4$

9) $8x^2 + 16x - 24$

10) $16x^2 - 8x + 4$

11) $6x^2 + 4x - 4$

12) $40x^3 + 24x^2 + 64x$

13) $27x^2 - 6x - 1$

14) $24x^2 + 10x - 25$

15) $35x^2 - 27x - 18$

16) $9x^2 + 12x - 32$

Solving Quadratic Equations

1) $x = -2, x = 4$

2) $x = -5, x = -8$

3) $x = -\frac{2}{3}, x = -3$

4) $x = -\frac{7}{4}, x = -\frac{5}{2}$

5) $x = 8, x = 3$

6) $x = -5, x = -2$

7) $x = 6, x = 4$

8) $x = -6, x = 3$

9) $x = \frac{1}{2}, x = -3$

10) $x = \frac{3}{5}, x = \frac{1}{3}$

11) $x = -5, x = -3$

Solving Systems of Equations by Substitution

1) (-1, 1)

2) (0, -3)

3) $(\frac{3}{2}, -8)$

4) (1, 2)

5) (4, 3)

6) (3, 2)

Solving Systems of Equations by Elimination

12) $(-\frac{6}{5}, 0)$

13) (1, -2)

14) (-4, -3)

15) (1, 1)

16) (-1 , 6)

17) (1, 1)

18) (2, 1)

19) No solution

Systems of Equations Word Problems

1) (2, 8)

2) (3, 4)

3) 34

4) boat: 26 mph, current: 2 mph

Day 6: Exponents, Roots and Statistics

Math Topics that you'll learn today:

- ✓ Multiplication Property of Exponents
- ✓ Division Property of Exponents
- ✓ Powers of Products and Quotients
- ✓ Zero and Negative Exponents
- ✓ Negative Exponents and Negative Bases
- ✓ Writing Scientific Notation
- ✓ Square Roots
- ✓ Mean, Median, Mode, and Range of the Given Data
- ✓ Bar Graph
- ✓ Box and Whisker Plots
- ✓ Stem– And– Leaf Plot
- ✓ The Pie Graph or Circle Graph
- ✓ Scatter Plots
- ✓ Probability

Mathematics is no more computation than typing is literature.

– John Allen Paulos

Multiplication Property of Exponents

Helpful *Hints*	**Exponents rules**	**Example:**
	$x^a \cdot x^b = x^{a+b}$ $x^a / x^b = x^{a-b}$	$(x^2y)^3 = x^6y^3$
	$1/x^b = x^{-b}$ $(x^a)^b = x^{a.b}$	
	$(xy)^a = x^a \cdot y^a$	

✎ **Simplify.**

1) $4^2 \cdot 4^2$ 4^4

2) $2 \cdot 2^2 \cdot 2^2$ $x^2 \cdot x^3 = x^{2+3}$

3) $3^2 \cdot 3^2$

4) $3x^3 \cdot x$

5) $12x^4 \cdot 3x$ $36x^5$

6) $6x \cdot 2x^2$

7) $5x^4 \cdot 5x^4$ $2^4 x^{2x4}$

8) $6x^2 \cdot 6x^3y^4$ 2^4 $16x^8$

9) $7x^2y^5 \cdot 9xy^3$

10) $7xy^4 \cdot 4x^3y^3$

11) $(2x^2)^2$ $2x^4 \rightarrow 4x^4$

12) $3x^5y^3 \cdot 8x^2y^3$

13) $7x^3 \cdot 10y^3x^5 \cdot 8yx^3$

14) $(x^4)^3$ x^{12}

15) $(2x^2)^4$ $2x^8 = 16x^8$

16) $(x^2)^3$ x^6

17) $(6x)^2$ $6x = 36x^2$

18) $3x^4y^5 \cdot 7x^2y^3$ $21x^6y^8$

Division Property of Exponents

Helpful	$\frac{x^a}{x^b} = x^{a-b}$, $x \neq 0$	Example:
Hints		$\frac{x^{12}}{x^5} = x^7$

✎**Simplify.**

1) $\frac{5^5}{5}$ 5^4

2) $\frac{3}{3^5}$ $4\,3^{-4}$ 3^4

3) $\frac{2^2}{2^3}$ 2^{-1} $\frac{1}{2^1}$

4) $\frac{2^4}{2^2}$

5) $\frac{x}{x^3}$

6) $\frac{3x^3}{9x^4}$

7) $\frac{2x^{-5}}{9x^{-2}}$

8) $\frac{21^8}{7x^3}$

9) $\frac{7x^6}{4x^7}$

10) $\frac{6x^2}{4x^3}$

11) $\frac{5x}{10x^3}$

12) $\frac{3x^3}{2x^5}$

13) $\frac{12x^3}{14^6}$

14) $\frac{12x^3}{9y^8}$

15) $\frac{25xy^4}{5x^6y^2}$ $\frac{5y^2}{x^5}$

16) $\frac{2x^4}{7x}$ $\frac{2}{7}x^3$

17) $\frac{16x^2y^8}{4x^3}$

18) $\frac{12x^4}{15x^7y^9}$

19) $\frac{12yx^4}{10yx^8}$

20) $\frac{16x^4y}{9x^8y^2}$

21) $\frac{5x^8}{20x^8}$

Powers of Products and Quotients

Helpful	For any nonzero numbers a and b and any integer x, $(ab)^x = a^x \cdot b^x$.	**Example:**
Hints		$(2x^2 \cdot y^3)^2 =$
		$4x^2 \cdot y^6$

✎ **Simplify.**

1) $(2x^3)^4$

$168x^{12}$

2) $(4xy^4)^2$

$16x^2y^8$

3) $(5x^4)^2$

4) $(11x^5)^2$

5) $(4x^2y^4)^4$

6) $(2x^4y^4)^3$

7) $(3x^2y^2)^2$

8) $(3x^4y^3)^4$

9) $(2x^6y^8)^2$

10) $(12x\ 3x)^3$

11) $(2x^9\ x^6)^3$

$8x^{27}x^{18} \rightarrow 8x^{45}$

12) $(5x^{10}y^3)^3$

13) $(4x^3\ x^2)^2$

14) $(3x^3\ 5x)^2$

15) $(10x^{11}y^3)^2$

16) $(9x^7\ y^5)^2$

17) $(4x^4y^6)^5$

18) $(4x^4)^2$

19) $(3x\ 4y^3)^2$

20) $(9x^2y)^3$

21) $(12x^2y^5)^2$

Zero and Negative Exponents

Helpful

Hints

A negative exponent simply means that the base is on the wrong side of the fraction line, so you need to flip the base to the other side. For instance, "x^{-2}" (pronounced as "ecks to the minus two") just means "x^2" but underneath, as in $\frac{1}{x^2}$.

Example:

$5^{-2} = \frac{1}{25}$

✎**Evaluate the following expressions.**

1) 8^{-2} $\frac{1}{8^2} = \frac{1}{64}$

2) 2^{-4}

3) 10^{-2}

4) 5^{-3}

5) 22^{-1}

6) 9^{-1}

7) 3^{-2}

8) 4^{-2}

9) 5^{-2}

10) 35^{-1} $\frac{1}{35}$

11) 6^{-3} $\frac{1}{6^3} = \frac{1}{216}$

12) 0^{15} $\frac{1}{0}$

13) 10^{-9}

14) 3^{-4}

15) 5^{-2}

16) 2^{-3}

17) 3^{-3}

18) 8^{-1}

19) 7^{-3}

20) 6^{-2}

21) $(\frac{2}{3})^{-2}$

22) $(\frac{1}{5})^{-3}$

23) $(\frac{1}{2})^{-8}$

24) $(\frac{2}{5})^{-3}$

Negative Exponents and Negative Bases

Helpful Hints	– Make the power positive. A negative exponent is the reciprocal of that number with a positive exponent. – The parenthesis is important! -5^{-2} is not the same as $(-5)^{-2}$ $-5^{-2} = -\frac{1}{5^2}$ and $(-5)^{-2} = +\frac{1}{5^2}$	**Example:** $2x^{-3} = \frac{2}{x^3}$

✎ **Simplify.**

1) -6^{-1} $-\frac{1}{6^1}$

2) $-4x^{-3}$

3) $-\frac{5x}{x^{-3}}$ $-5^{-2} \rightarrow -\frac{1}{5^2}$

4) $-\frac{a^{-3}}{b^{-2}}$ $-\frac{a^{-3}}{b^{-2}} \quad \frac{b^2}{a^3} \quad \frac{a^3}{b^2}$

5) $-\frac{5}{x^{-3}}$

6) $\frac{7b}{-9c^{-4}}$

7) $-\frac{5n^{-2}}{10^{-3}}$

8) $\frac{4ab^{-2}}{-3c^{-2}}$

9) $-12x^2y^{-3}$

10) $\left(-\frac{1}{3}\right)^{-2}$

11) $\left(-\frac{3}{4}\right)^{-2}$

12) $\left(\frac{3a}{2c}\right)^{-2}$

13) $\left(-\frac{5x}{3y}\right)^{-3}$

14) $-\frac{2x}{a^{-4}}$

Writing Scientific Notation

Helpful	– It is used to write very big or very small numbers in decimal form.
Hints	– In scientific notation all numbers are written in the form of:

$$m \times 10^n$$

Decimal notation	Scientific notation
5	5×10^0
−25,000	-2.5×10^4
0.5	5×10^{-1}
2,122.456	$2,122456 \times 10^3$

✎ **Write each number in scientific notation.**

1) 91×10^3

9.1×10^4

2) 60

6.0×10^1

3) 2000000

20.00000×10^5

2.00000×10^6

4) 0.0000006

5) 354000

6) 0.000325

7) 2.5

8) 0.00023

9) 56000000

10) 2000000

11) 78000000

12) 0.0000022

13) 0.00012

14) 0.004

15) 78

16) 1600

17) 1450

18) 130000

19) 60

20) 0.113

21) 0.02

Square Roots

Helpful	— A square root of x is a number r whose square is: $r^2 = x$	Example:
Hints	r is a square root of x.	$\sqrt{4} = 2$

✎ **Find the value each square root.**

1) $\sqrt{1}$
    1

2) $\sqrt{4}$
    2

3) $\sqrt{9}$
    3

4) $\sqrt{25}$
    5

5) $\sqrt{16}$
    4

6) $\sqrt{49}$
    7

7) $\sqrt{36}$
    6

8) $\sqrt{0}$
    0

9) $\sqrt{64}$
    8

10) $\sqrt{81}$
    9

11) $\sqrt{121}$
    11

12) $\sqrt{225}$
    25

13) $\sqrt{144}$
    12

14) $\sqrt{100}$
    10

15) $\sqrt{256}$
    16

16) $\sqrt{289}$
    17

17) $\sqrt{324}$
    18

18) $\sqrt{400}$
    20

19) $\sqrt{900}$
    30

20) $\sqrt{529}$

21) $\sqrt{90}$
    $3\sqrt{10}$

Mean, Median, Mode, and Range of the Given Data

Helpful		Example:
	- Mean: $\dfrac{\text{sum of the data}}{\text{of data entires}}$	
	- Mode: value in the list that appears most often	22, 16, 12, 9, 7, 6, 4, 6
Hints	- Range: largest value − smallest value	
		Mean = 10.25
		Mod = 6
		Range = 18

✍ *Find Mean, Median, Mode, and Range of the Given Data.*

1) 7, 2, 5, 1, 1, 2

2) 2, 2, 2, 3, 6, 3, 7, 4

3) 9, 4, 3, 1, 7, 9, 4, 6, 4

4) 8, 4, 2, 4, 3, 2, 4, 5

5) 8, 5, 7, 5, 7, 9, 8

6) 5, 1, 4, 4, 9, 2, 9, 2, 5, 1

7) 4, 1, 5, 9, 7, 7, 5, 4, 3, 5

8) 7, 5, 4, 9, 6, 7, 7, 5, 2

9) 2, 5, 5, 6, 2, 4, 7, 6, 4, 9

10) 10, 5, 2, 5, 4, 5, 8, 10

11) 5, 1, 5, 2, 2

12) 2, 3, 5, 9, 6

Box and Whisker Plots

Box–and–whisker plots display data including quartiles.

- IQR – interquartile range shows the difference from Q1 to Q3.
- Extreme Values are the smallest and largest values in a data set.

Example:

73, 84, 86, 95, 68, 67, 100, 94, 77, 80, 62, 79

Maximum: 100, Minimum: 62, Q_1: 70.5, Q_2: 79.5, Q_3: 90

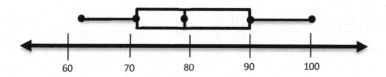

✎ *Make box and whisker plots for the given data.*

11, 17, 22, 18, 23, 2, 3, 16, 21, 7, 8, 15, 5

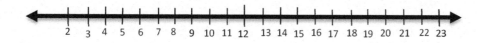

Bar Graph

Helpful	– A bar graph is a chart that presents data with bars in different heights to match with the values of the data. The bars can be graphed horizontally or vertically.
Hints	

✎ **Graph the given information as a bar graph.**

Day	Hot dogs sold
Monday	90
Tuesday	70
Wednesday	30
Thursday	20
Friday	60

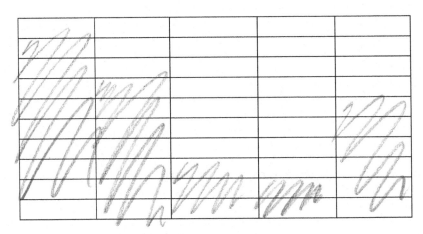

Monday   Tuesday   Wednesday   Thursday   Friday

Stem–And–Leaf Plot

Helpful	– Stem–and–leaf plots display the frequency of the values in a data set.
Hints	– We can make a frequency distribution table for the values, or we can use a stem–and–leaf plot.

Example:

56, 58, 42, 48, 66, 64, 53, 69, 45, 72

Stem	leaf		
4	2	5	8
5	3	6	8
6	4	6	9
7	2		

✍ *Make stem ad leaf plots for the given data.*

1) 74, 88, 97, 72, 79, 86, 95, 79, 83, 91

Stem | Leaf plot

2) 37, 48, 26, 33, 49, 26, 19, 26, 48

Stem | Leaf plot

3) 58, 41, 42, 67, 54, 65, 65, 54, 69, 53

Stem | Leaf plot

The Pie Graph or Circle Graph

Helpful	A Pie Chart is a circle chart divided into sectors, each sector represents the relative size of each value.
Hints	

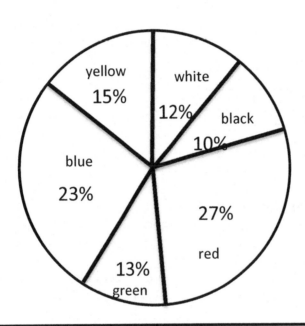

Favorite colors

1) Which color is the most?

2) What percentage of pie graph is yellow?

3) Which color is the least?

4) What percentage of pie graph is blue?

5) What percentage of pie graph is green?

Scatter Plots

Helpful	A Scatter (xy) Plot shows the values with points that represent the relationship between two sets of data.
Hints	– The horizontal values are usually x and vertical data is y.

✎ *Construct a scatter plot.*

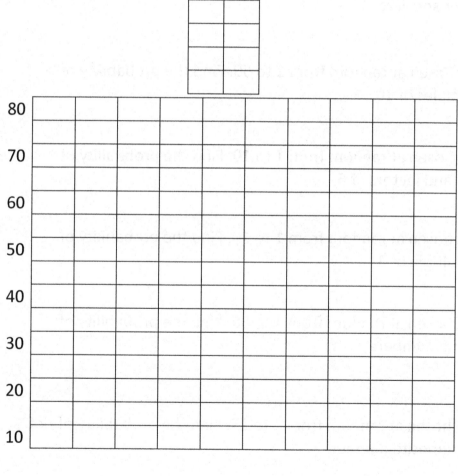

Probability Problems

Helpful	- Probability is the likelihood of something happening in the future. It is expressed as a number between zero (can never happen) to 1 (will always happen).	**Example:**
Hints	- Probability can be expressed as a fraction, a decimal, or a percent.	Probability of a flipped coins turns up 'heads' Is $0.5 = \dfrac{1}{2}$

✎ **Solve.**

1) A number is chosen at random from 1 to 10. Find the probability of selecting a 4 or smaller.

$$\frac{4}{10} = \frac{2}{5}$$

2) A number is chosen at random from 1 to 50. Find the probability of selecting multiples of 10.

$$\frac{5}{50}$$

3) A number is chosen at random from 1 to 10. Find the probability of selecting of 4 and <u>factors of 6.</u>

$1\ 2\ 3\ 4$

$\dfrac{4}{10} = \dfrac{2}{5}$

$\dfrac{5}{10} = \dfrac{1}{2}$ 4. $1.2.3.6$ 1×6

4) A number is chosen at random from 1 to 10. Find the probability of selecting a multiple of 3.

$3\ 6\ 9$ $\dfrac{3}{10}$

5) A number is chosen at random from 1 to 50. Find the probability of selecting prime numbers.

6) A number is chosen at random from 1 to 25. Find the probability of not selecting a composite number.

Answers of Worksheets – Day 6

Multiplication Property of Exponents

1) 4^4

2) 2^5

3) 3^4

4) $3x^4$

5) $36x^5$

6) $12x^3$

7) $25x^8$

8) $36x^5y^4$

9) $63x^3y^8$

10) $28x^4y^7$

11) $4x^4$

12) $24x^7y^6$

13) $560x^{11}y^4$

14) x^{12}

15) $16x^8$

16) x^6

17) $36x^2$

18) $21x^6y^8$

Division Property of Exponents

1) 5^4

2) $\dfrac{1}{3^4}$

3) $\dfrac{1}{2}$

4) 2^2

5) $\dfrac{1}{x^2}$

6) $\dfrac{1}{3x}$

7) $\dfrac{2}{9x^3}$

8) $3x^5$

9) $\dfrac{7}{4x}$

10) $\dfrac{3}{2x}$

11) $\dfrac{1}{2x^2}$

12) $\dfrac{3}{2x^2}$

13) $\dfrac{6}{7x^3}$

14) $\dfrac{4x^3}{3y^8}$

15) $\dfrac{5y^2}{x^5}$

16) $\dfrac{2x^3}{7}$

17) $\dfrac{4y^8}{x}$

18) $\dfrac{4}{5x^3y^9}$

19) $\dfrac{6}{5x^4}$

20) $\dfrac{16}{9x^4y}$

21) $\dfrac{1}{4}$

Powers of Products and Quotients

1) $16x^{12}$

2) $16x^2y^8$

3) $25x^8$

4) $121x^{10}$

5) $256x^8y^{16}$

6) $8x^{12}y^{12}$

7) $9x^4y^4$

8) $81x^{16}y^{12}$

9) $4x^{12}y^{16}$

10) $46,656x^6$

11) $8x^{45}$

12) $125x^{30}y^9$

13) $16x^{10}$

14) $225x^8$

15) $100x^{22}y^6$

16) $81x^{14}y^{10}$

17) $1,024x^{20}y^{30}$

18) $16x^8$

19) $144x^2y^6$

20) $729x^6y^3$

21) $144x^4y^{10}$

Zero and Negative Exponents

1) $\frac{1}{64}$

2) $\frac{1}{16}$

3) $\frac{1}{100}$

4) $\frac{1}{125}$

5) $\frac{1}{22}$

6) $\frac{1}{9}$

7) $\frac{1}{9}$

8) $\frac{1}{16}$

9) $\frac{1}{25}$

10) $\frac{1}{35}$

11) $\frac{1}{216}$

12) 0

13) $\frac{1}{1000000000}$

14) $\frac{1}{81}$

15) $\frac{1}{25}$

16) $\frac{1}{8}$

17) $\frac{1}{27}$

18) $\frac{1}{8}$

19) $\frac{1}{343}$

20) $\frac{1}{36}$

21) $\frac{9}{4}$

22) 125

23) 256

24) $\frac{125}{8}$

Negative Exponents and Negative Bases

1) $-\frac{1}{6}$

2) $-\frac{4}{x^3}$

3) $-5x^4$

4) $-\frac{b^2}{a^3}$

5) $-5x^3$

6) $-\frac{7bc^4}{9}$

7) $-\frac{p^3}{2n^2}$

8) $-\frac{4ac^2}{3b^2}$

9) $-\frac{12^2}{y^3}$

10) 9

11) $\frac{16}{9}$

12) $\frac{4c^2}{9a^2}$

13) $-\frac{27\,^3z^3}{125x^3}$

14) $-2xa^4$

Writing Scientific Notation

1) 9.1×10^4

2) 6×10^1

3) 2×10^6

4) 6×10^{-7}

5) 3.54×10^5

6) 3.25×10^{-4}

7) 2.5×10^0

8) 2.3×10^{-4}

9) 5.6×10^7

10) 2×10^6

11) 7.8×10^7

12) 2.2×10^{-6}

13) 1.2×10^{-4}

14) 4×10^{-3}

15) 7.8×10^1

16) 1.6×10^3

17) 1.45×10^3

18) 1.3×10^5

19) 6×10^1

20) 1.13×10^{-1}

21) 2×10^{-2}

Square Roots

1) 1	8) 0	15) 16
2) 2	9) 8	16) 17
3) 3	10) 9	17) 18
4) 5	11) 11	18) 20
5) 4	12) 15	19) 30
6) 7	13) 12	20) 23
7) 6	14) 10	21) $3\sqrt{10}$

Mean, Median, Mode, and Range of the Given Data

1) mean: 3, median: 2, mode: 1, 2, range: 6
2) mean: 3.625, median: 3, mode: 2, range: 5
3) mean: 5.22, median: 4, mode: 4, range: 8
4) mean: 4, median: 4, mode: 4, range: 6
5) mean: 7, median: 7, mode: 5, 7, 8, range: 4
6) mean: 4.2, median: 4, mode: 1,2,4,5,9, range: 8
7) mean: 5, median: 5, mode: 5, range: 8
8) mean: 5.78, median: 6, mode: 7, range: 7
9) mean: 5, median: 5, mode: 2, 4, 5, 6, range: 7
10) mean: 6.125, median: 5, mode: 5, range: 8
11) mean: 3, median: 2, mode: 2, 5, range: 4
12) mean: 5, median: 5, mode: none, range: 7

Box and Whisker Plots

11, 17, 22, 18, 23, 2, 3, 16, 21, 7, 8, 15, 5

Maximum: 23, Minimum: 2, Q_1: 2, Q_2: 12.5, Q_3: 19.5

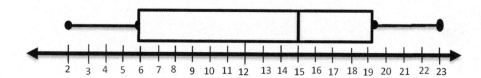

Bar Graph

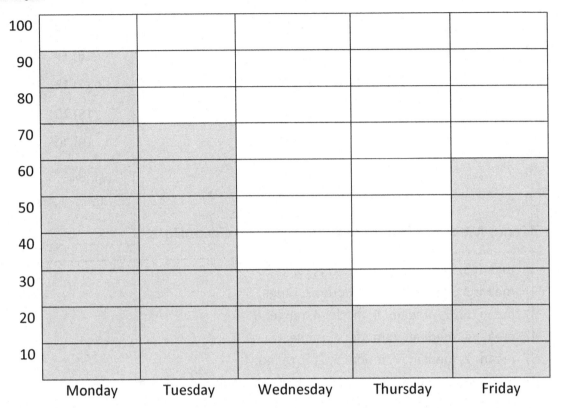

Stem–And–Leaf Plot

1)

Stem	leaf
7	2 4 9 9
8	3 6 8
9	1 5 7

2)

Stem	leaf
1	9
2	6 6 6
3	3 7
4	8 8 9

3)

Stem	leaf
4	1 2
5	3 4 4 8
6	5 5 7 9

The Pie Graph or Circle Graph

1) red
2) 15%

3) black
4) 23%

5) 13%

Scatter Plots

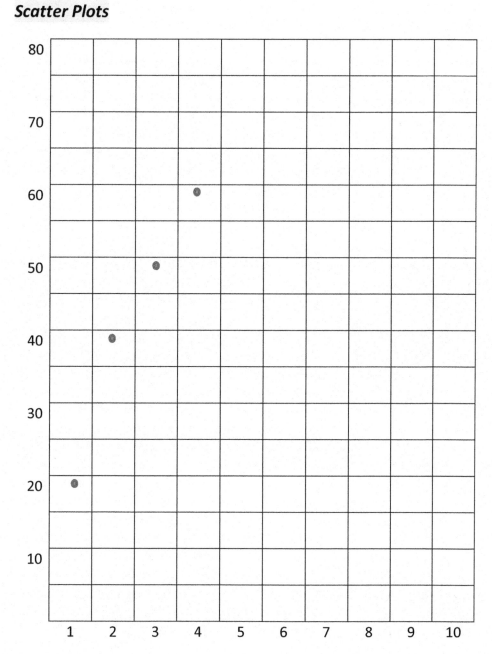

Probability Problems

1) $\frac{2}{5}$

2) $\frac{1}{10}$

3) $\frac{1}{5}$

4) $\frac{3}{10}$

5) $\frac{3}{10}$

6) $\frac{2}{5}$

Day 7: Geometry

Math Topics that you'll learn today:

- ✓ The Pythagorean Theorem
- ✓ Area of Triangles
- ✓ Perimeter of Polygons
- ✓ Area and Circumference of Circles
- ✓ Area of Squares, Rectangles, and Parallelograms
- ✓ Area of Trapezoids
- ✓ Volume of Cubes
- ✓ Volume of Rectangle Prisms
- ✓ Surface Area of Cubes
- ✓ Surface Area of a Prism
- ✓ Volume of a Cylinder
- ✓ Surface Area of a Cylinder

Mathematics is, as it were, a sensuous logic, and relates to philosophy as do the arts, music, and plastic

art to poetry. — K. Shegel

The Pythagorean Theorem

Helpful Hints

– In any right triangle:

$$a^2 + b^2 = c^2$$

Example:

Missing side = 5

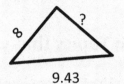

9.43

✎ **Do the following lengths form a right triangle?**

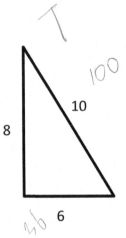
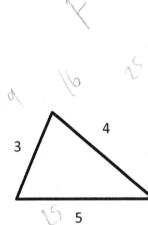
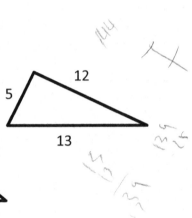

✎ **Find each missing length to the nearest tenth.**

4)

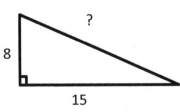

5)   6)

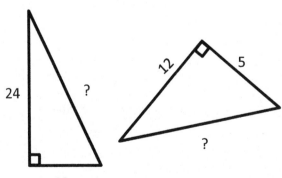

Area of Triangles

Helpful $\text{Area} = \frac{1}{2} (base \times height)$

Hints

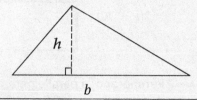

✎**Find the area of each.**

1)

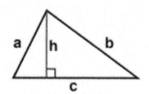

c = 9 mi

h = 3.7 mi

2)

s = 14 m

h = 12.2 m

3)

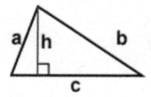

a = 5 m

b = 11 m

c = 14 m

h = 4 m

4)

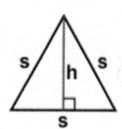

s = 10 m

h = 8.6 m

Perimeter of Polygons

Helpful

Hints

Perimeter of a square = 4s

Perimeter of a rectangle

= $2(l + w)$

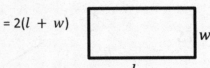

Perimeter of trapezoid

= a + b + c + d

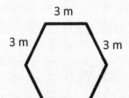

Perimeter of Pentagon = 6a

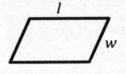

Perimeter of a parallelogram = 2(l + w)

Example:

P = 18

3 m

3 m   3 m

✍️ *Find the perimeter of each shape.*

1)
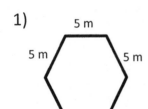
5 m

5 m   5 m

2)
15 mm

15 mm   15mm

15 mm

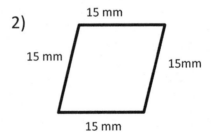

3)
12 ft   12 ft

12 ft   12 ft

4)
18 in

12 in   12 in

18 in

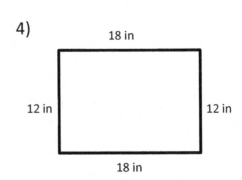

Area and Circumference of Circles

Helpful Hints	Area = πr² Circumference = 2πr 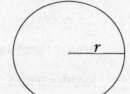	Example: If the radius of a circle is 3, then: Area = 28.27 Circumference = 18.85

✎ **Find the area and circumference of each.** (π = 3.14)

1)

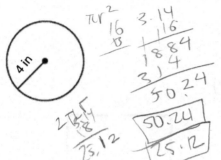

πr^2
16   3.14
8   116
      1884
      314
      50.24

2$\frac{\pi}{8}$5.4
23.12   50.24
         25.12

2)

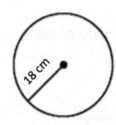

3)

4)

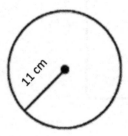

5)

6)

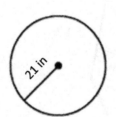

Area of Squares, Rectangles, and Parallelograms

Helpful

Hints

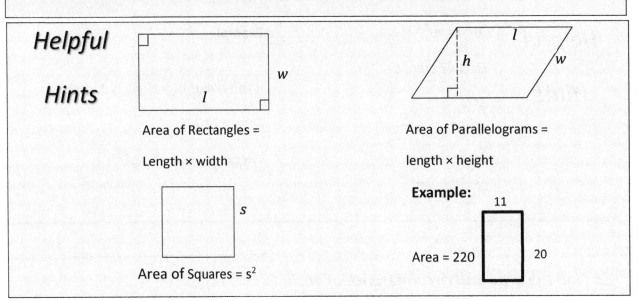

Area of Rectangles =

Length × width

Area of Squares = s²

Area of Parallelograms =

length × height

Example:

Area = 220

🖎 *Find the area of each.*

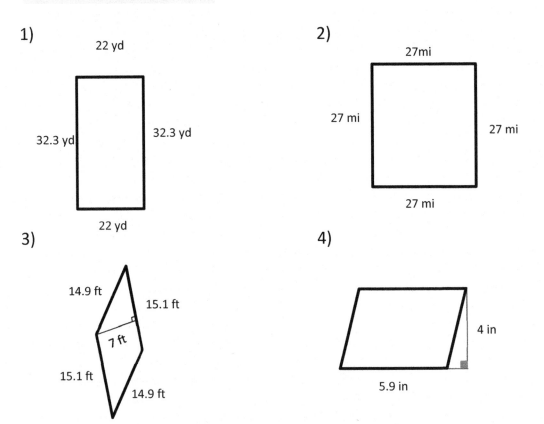

1)

22 yd

32.3 yd   32.3 yd

22 yd

2)

27mi

27 mi   27 mi

27 mi

3)

14.9 ft

15.1 ft

7 ft

15.1 ft

14.9 ft

4)

4 in

5.9 in

Area of Trapezoids

Helpful

Hints

$A = \frac{1}{2}h(b_1 + b_2)$

Example:

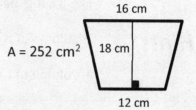

A = 252 cm²

16 cm

18 cm

12 cm

✎ **Calculate the area for each trapezoid.**

1)

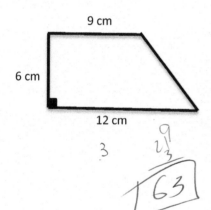

9 cm

6 cm

12 cm

3 $2\frac{9}{3}$

$\boxed{63}$

2)

14 m

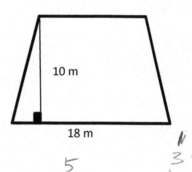

10 m

18 m

5 $3\ 2$ $\frac{2}{5}$

$\boxed{160}$

3)

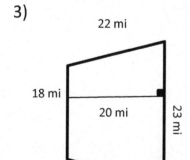

22 mi

18 mi

20 mi

23 mi

22 mi

4)

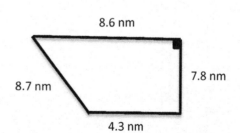

8.6 nm

8.7 nm

7.8 nm

4.3 nm

Volume of Cubes

Helpful	– Volume is the measure of the amount of space inside of a solid figure, like a cube, ball, cylinder or pyramid.
Hints	– Volume of a cube = (one side)^3
	– Volume of a rectangle prism: Length × Width × Height

✎ **Find the volume of each.**

1)

2)
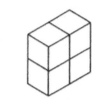

3)

4)
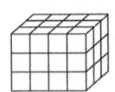

24 ⨳ 16 + 4

5)
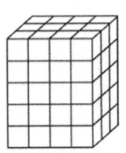

6)
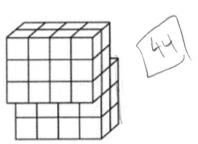

44

Volume of Rectangle Prisms

Helpful	Volume of rectangle prism	Example:
		$10 \times 5 \times 8 = 400$
Hints	length × width × height	

✎ *Find the volume of each of the rectangular prisms.*

1)

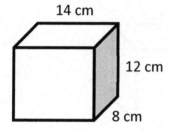

14 cm
12 cm
8 cm

2)

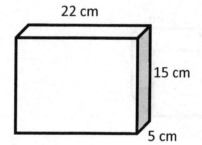

22 cm
15 cm
5 cm

3)

8 m
8 m
8 m

4)

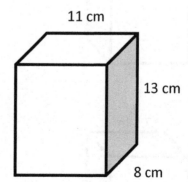

11 cm
13 cm
8 cm

Surface Area of Cubes

Helpful

Hints

Surface Area of a cube =

6 × (one side of the cube)^2

Example:

$6 \times 4^2 = 96m^3$

4 m

4 m

4 m

✎ *Find the surface of each cube.*

1)

6 mm

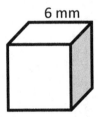

2)

9 mm

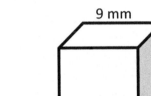

3)

10 cm

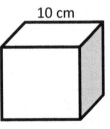

4)

8 m

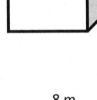

5)

7.5 in

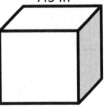

6)

11.3 ft

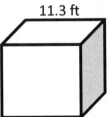

Surface Area of a Rectangle Prism

Helpful

Hints

Surface Area of a Rectangle Prism Formula:

SA =2 [(width × length) + (height × length) + width × height)]

✎**Find the surface of each prism.**

1)

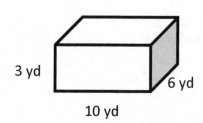

3 yd

6 yd

10 yd

2)

7 mm

7 mm

7 mm

3)

8 in

13.2 in

6.7 in

4)

17 cm

17 cm

11 cm

Volume of a Cylinder

Helpful

Hints

Volume of Cylinder Formula = π(radius)² × height

π = 3.14

✎ **Find the volume of each cylinder.** (π = 3.14)

1)

2)

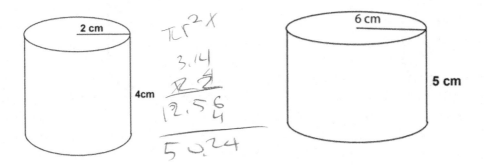

3)

4)

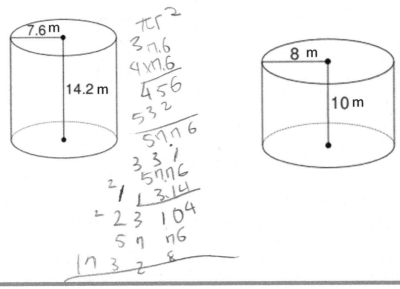

www.EffortlessMath.com

Surface Area of a Cylinder

<table>
<tr>
<td>

Helpful

Hints

</td>
<td>

Surface area of a cylinder

$SA = 2\pi r^2 + 2\pi rh$

</td>
<td>

Example:

Surface area

= 1727

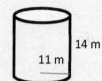

14 m

11 m

</td>
</tr>
</table>

Find the surface of each cylinder. ($\pi = 3.14$)

1)

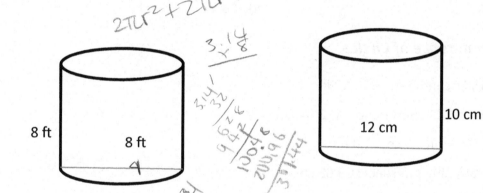

8 ft   8 ft

2)

12 cm   10 cm

3)

16 in

18 in

4)

12 yd

8 yd

Answers of Worksheets – Day 7

The Pythagorean Theorem

1) yes

2) yes

3) yes

4) 17

5) 26

6) 13

Area of Triangles

1) 16.65 mi^2

2) 56 m^2

3) 85.4 m^2

4) 43 m^2

Perimeter of Polygons

1) 30 m

2) 60 mm

3) 48 ft

4) 60 in

Area and Circumference of Circles

1) Area: 50.24 in^2, Circumference: 25.12 in

2) Area: 1,017.36 cm^2, Circumference: 113.04 cm

3) Area: 78.5 m^2, Circumference: 31.4 m

4) Area: 379.94 cm^2, Circumference: 69.08 cm

5) Area: 200.96 km^2, Circumference: 50.2 km

6) Area: 1,384.74 km^2, Circumference: 131.88 km

Area of Squares, Rectangles, and Parallelograms

1) 710.6 yd^2

2) 729 mi^2

3) 105.7 ft^2

4) 23.6 in^2

Area of Trapezoids

1) 63 cm^2

2) 192 m^2

3) 451 mi^2

4) 50.31 nm^2

Volumes of Cubes

1) 8

2) 4

3) 5

4) 36

5) 60

6) 44

Volume of Rectangle Prisms

1) 1344 cm^3

2) 1650 cm^3

3) 512 m^3

4) 1144 cm^3

Surface Area of a Cube

1) 216 mm^2

2) 486 mm^2

3) 600 cm^2

4) 384 m^2

5) 337.5 in^2

6) 766.14 ft^2

Surface Area of a Prism

1) 216 yd^2

2) 294 mm^2

3) 495.28 in^2

4) 1326 cm^2

Volume of a Cylinder

1) 50.24 cm^3

2) 565.2 cm^3

3) 2,575.403 m^3

4) 2009.6 m^3

Surface Area of a Cylinder

1) 301.44 ft^2

2) 602.88 cm^2

3) 1413 in^2

4) 401.92 yd^2

Time to Test

Time to refine your skill with a practice examination

Take a practice SSAT UPPER LEVEL Math Test to simulate the test day experience. After you've finished, score your test using the answer key.

Before You Start

- You'll need a pencil and a timer to take the test.

- After you've finished the test, review the answer key to see where you went go.

- You will receive 1 point for every correct answer and you will lose $\frac{1}{4}$ point for each incorrect answer. There is no penalty for skipping a question.

SSAT UPPER LEVEL Math
Practice Test 1

Section 1

25 questions

Total time for this section: 30 Minutes

You may NOT use a calculator for this test.

1) If $\frac{25}{A} + 1 = 6$, then $25 + A = ?$

$\frac{25}{A \times A} + 1 = 6$

$25 + 1 = 6A$

$26 = 6A$
$\frac{26}{6} = \frac{6A}{6}$

$6\overline{)26}$
$\underline{24}$
4

$\frac{26}{6} = A$

A. 6

B. 1

C. 25

D. 30

E. 0

2) A school wants to give each of its 20 top students a football ball. If the balls are in boxes of three, how many boxes of balls they need to purchase?

A. 3

B. 5

C. 6

D. 7

E. 20

3) How many tiles of 8 cm² is needed to cover a floor of dimension 6 cm by 24 cm?

A. 6

B. 12

C. 18

D. 24

E. 36

$\begin{array}{r} {\scriptstyle 2} \\ 24 \\ \times\ 6 \\ \hline 144 \end{array}$

$\begin{array}{r} 18 \\ 8\overline{)144} \\ \underline{-8} \\ 64 \end{array}$

4) A shaft rotates 300 times in 8 seconds. How many times does it rotate in 12 seconds?

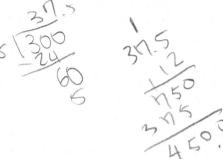

    A. 450

    B. 300

    C. 200

    D. 150

    E. 100

5) Which of the following statements is correct, according to the graph below?

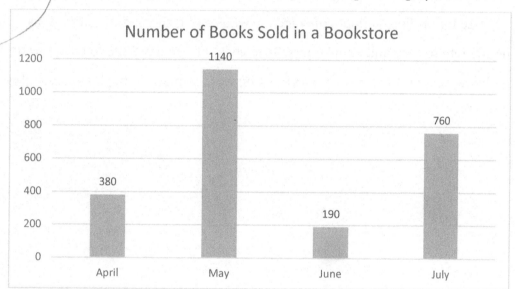

Number of Books Sold in a Bookstore

A. Number of books sold in April was twice the number of books sold in July.

B. Number of books sold in July was less than half the number of books sold in May.

C. Number of books sold in June was half the number of books sold in April.

D. Number of books sold in July was equal to the number of books sold in April plus the number of books sold in June.

E. More books were sold in April than in July.

6) What is the value of the sum of the tens and thousandths in number 2,517.89451?

    A. 16

    B. 11

    C. 9

    D. 14

    E. 5

7) Jack earns $616 for his first 44 hours of work in a week and is then paid 1.5 times his regular hourly rate for any additional hours. This week, Jack needs $826 to pay his rent, bills and other expenses. How many hours must he work to make enough money in this week?

    A. 40

    B. 48

    C. 50

    D. 53

    E. 54

8) $12.124 \div 0.002$?

    A. 6.0620

    B. 60.620

    C. 606.20

    D. 6,062.0

    E. 600620

9) $\dfrac{1\frac{3}{4}+\frac{1}{3}}{2\frac{1}{2}-\frac{15}{8}}$ is approximately equal to.

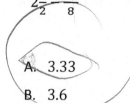

A. 3.33

B. 3.6

C. 5.67

D. 6.33

E. 6.67

10) If 150 % of a number is 75, then what is the 90 % of that number?

A. 45

B. 50

C. 60

D. 70

E. 85

11) If $x \blacksquare y = \sqrt{x^2 + y}$, what is the value of $5 \blacksquare 11$?

A. $\sqrt{126}$

B. 6

C. 4

D. 3

E. 2

12) There are three equal tanks of water. If 2/5 of a tank contains 200 liters of water, what is the capacity of the three tanks of water together?

A. 1500

B. 500

C. 240

D. 80

E. 200

13) What is the answer of $7.5 \div 0.15$?

A. $\frac{1}{50}$

B. $\frac{1}{5}$

C. 5

D. 50

E. 500

14) The average weight of 18 girls in a class is 60 kg and the average weight of 32 boys in the same class is 62 kg. What is the average weight of all the 50 students in that class?

A. 60

B. 61.28

C. 61.68

D. 61.9

E. 62.20

15) If $1 \leq x < 4$, what is the minimum value of the following expression?

$$2x + 1$$

A. 8

B. 5

C. 3

D. 2

E. 1

16) What is the value of x in the following figure?

A. 150

B. 145

C. 125

D. 115

E. 105

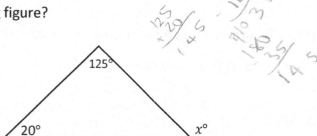

17) Michelle and Alec can finish a job together in 100 minutes. If Michelle can do the job by herself in 5 hours, how many minutes does it take Alec to finish the job?

A. 120

B. 150

C. 180

D. 200

E. 220

18) The sum of six different negative integers is −70. If the smallest of these integers is −15, what is the largest possible value of one of the other five integers?

A. −14

B. −10

C. −5

D. −4

E. −1

41

19) David's current age is 42 years, and Ava's current age is 6 years old. In how many years David's age will be 4 times Ava's age?

A. 4

B. 6

C. 8

D. 10

E. 14

20) Two-kilograms apple and three-kilograms orange cost $26.4. If one-kilogram apple costs $4.2 how much does one-kilogram orange cost?

A. $9

B. $6

C. $5.5

D. $5

E. $4

21) What is the slope of a line that is perpendicular to the line $4x - 2y = 12$?

A. -2

B. $-\dfrac{1}{2}$

C. 4

D. 12

E. 14

$\dfrac{-2y}{-2} = \dfrac{-4x}{-2} + \dfrac{12}{-2}$

$y = 2x$

22) A cruise line ship left Port A and traveled 80 miles due west and then 150 miles due north. At this point, what is the shortest distance from the cruise to port A?

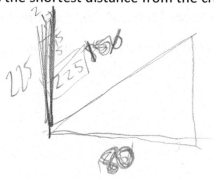

A. 70 miles

B. 80 miles

C. 150 miles

D. 170 miles

E. 230 miles

23) A football team won exactly 80% of the games it played during last session. Which of the following could be the total number of games the team played last season?

A. 49

B. 35

C. 32

D. 16

E. 12

24) The width of a box is one third of its length. The height of the box is one third of its width. If the length of the box is 27 cm, what is the volume of the box?

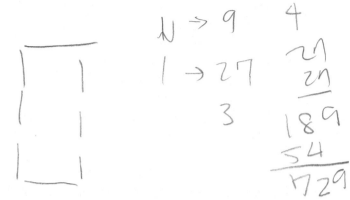

A. 81 cm^3

B. 162 cm^3

C. 243 cm^3

D. 729 cm^3

E. 1880 cm^3

25) The Jackson Library is ordering some bookshelves. If x is the number of bookshelf the library wants to order, which each costs $100 and there is a one-time delivery charge of $800, which of the following represents the total cost, in dollar, per bookshelf?

A. $100x + 800$

B. $100 + 800x$

C. $\dfrac{100x + 800}{100}$

D. $\dfrac{100x + 800}{x}$

E. $100x - 800$

SSAT UPPER LEVEL Math
Practice Test 1

Section 2

25 questions

Total time for this section: 30 Minutes

You may NOT use a calculator for this test.

1) There are 11 marbles in the bag A and 17 marbles in the bag B. If the sum of the marbles in both bags will be shared equally between two children, how many marbles bag A has less than the marbles that each child will receive?

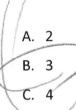

14

A. 2

B. 3

C. 4

D. 5

E. 6

2) When number 91,501 is divided by 305, the result is closest to?

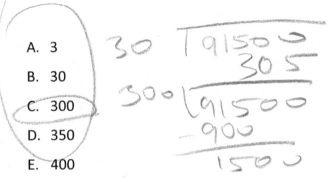

A. 3

B. 30

C. 300

D. 350

E. 400

3) If Jason's mark is k more than Alex, and Jason's mark is 16, which of the following can be Alex's mark?

$16 - k$

A. $16 + k$

B. $k - 16$

C. $\frac{k}{16}$

D. $16k$

E. $16 - k$

4) To paint a wall with the area of $36m^2$, how many liters of paint do we need if each liter of paint is enough to paint a wall with dimension of $72\ cm \times 100\ cm$?

A. 50

B. 100

C. 150

D. 200

E. 250

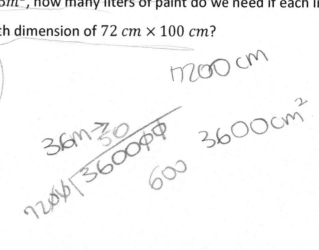

5) If the perimeter of the following figure be 20, what is the value of x?

A. 2

B. 3

C. 6

D. 9

E. 12

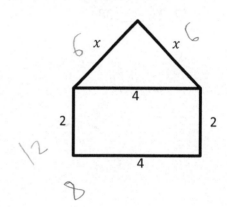

6) $750 - 7\frac{7}{15} = ?$

A. $742\frac{7}{15}$

B. $742\frac{8}{15}$

C. $743\frac{1}{15}$

D. $743\frac{8}{15}$

E. $744\frac{1}{15}$

7) Which of the following expression is not equal to 5?

   A. $10 \times \frac{1}{2}$

   B. $25 \times \frac{1}{5}$

   C. $2 \times \frac{5}{2}$

   D. $6 \times \frac{5}{6}$

   E. $5 \times \frac{1}{5}$

8) What is the missing term in the given sequence?

   2, 3, 5, 8, 12, 17, 23, ___, 38

   A. 24

   B. 26

   C. 27

   D. 28

   E. 30

9) A driver rests one hour and 12 minutes for every 4 hours driving. How many minutes will he rest if he drives 20 hours?

   A. 3 hours and 36 minutest

   B. 4 hours and 12 minutest

   C. 4 hours and 45 minutest

   D. 5 hours and 36 minutest

   E. 6 hours

10) The price of a sofa is decreased by 25% to $420. What was its original price?

A. $480

B. $520

C. $560

D. $600

E. $800

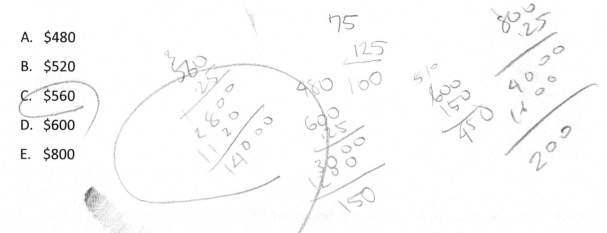

Questions 11 to 12 are based on the following data

A library has 840 books that include Mathematics, Physics, Chemistry, English and History.

Use following graph to answer questions 15 to 17.

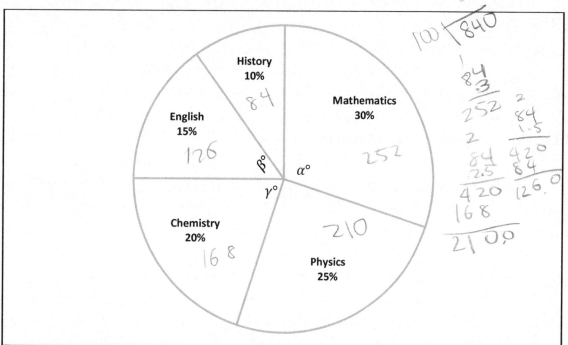

11) What is the product of the number of Mathematics and number of English books?

A. 21168

B. 31752

C. 26460

D. 17640

E. 35280

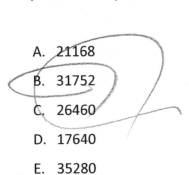
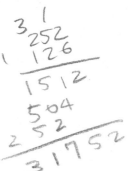

12) What are the values of angle α and β respectively?

A. 90°, 54°

B. 120°, 36°

C. 120°, 45°

D. 108°, 54°

E. 108°, 45°

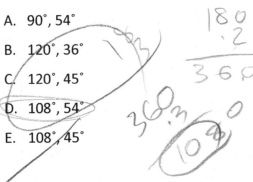

13) If $3y + 5 < 29$, then y could be equal to?

A. 15

B. 12

C. 10.5

D. 8

E. 2.5

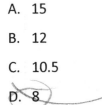

14) The capacity of a red box is 20% bigger than the capacity of a blue box. If the red box can hold 30 equal sized books, how many of the same books can the blue box hold?

A. 9

B. 15

C. 21

D. 25

E. 30

15) Find the perimeter of following shape.

A. 21

B. 22

C. 23

D. 24

E. 25

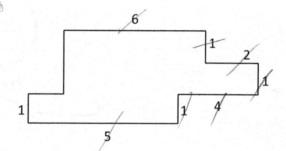

16) There are 50.2 liters of gas in a car fuel tank. In the first week and second week of April, the car uses 5.82 and 25.9 liters of gas respectively. If the car was park in the third week of April and 10.31 liters of gas will be added to the fuel tank, how many liters of gas are in the fuel tank of the car?

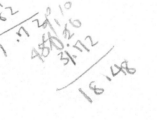

A. 21.41

B. 25.9

C. 27

D. 28.79

E. 71.61

17) If $3x + y = 25$ and $x - z = 14$, what is the value of x?

   A. 0

   B. 5

   C. 10

   D. 20

   E. it cannot be determined from the information given

18) What is the average of circumference of figure A and area of figure B? ($\pi = 3$)

   A. 54

   B. 53

   C. 52

   D. 51

   E. 50

Figure A

Figure B

19) If $a \times b$ is divisible by 3, which of the following expression must also be divisible by 3?

   A. 0

   B. $3a - b$

   C. $a - 3b$

   D. $\frac{a}{b}$

   E. $4 \times a \times b$

20) If the area of the following rectangular ABCD is 100, and E is the midpoint of AB, what is

the area of the shaded part?

A. 25

B. 50

C. 75

D. 80

E. 100

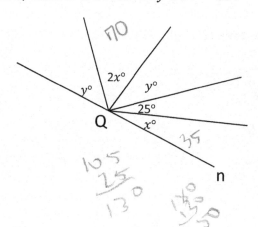

21) In the following figure, point Q lies on line n, what is the value of y if $x = 35$?

A. 15

B. 25

C. 35

D. 45

E. 55

22) A number is chosen at random from 1 to 25. Find the probability of not selecting a

composite number. (A composite number is a number that is divisible by itself, 1 and at

least one other whole number)

A. $\dfrac{1}{25}$

B. $\dfrac{2}{5}$

C. $\dfrac{9}{25}$

D. 1

E. 0

23) $712 \div 3 =?$

A. $\dfrac{700}{3} \times \dfrac{10}{3} \times \dfrac{2}{3}$

B. $700 + \dfrac{10}{3} + \dfrac{2}{3}$

 C. $\dfrac{700}{3} + \dfrac{10}{3} + \dfrac{2}{3}$

D. $\dfrac{700}{3} \div \dfrac{10}{3} \div \dfrac{2}{3}$

E. $\dfrac{7}{3} + \dfrac{1}{3} + \dfrac{2}{3}$

24) If a gas tank can hold 25 gallons, how many gallons does it contain when it is $\dfrac{2}{5}$ full?

A. 125

B. 62.5

C. 50

D. 10

E. 5

25) Which of the following could be the value of x if $\dfrac{5}{9} + x > 2$?

A. $\dfrac{1}{2}$

B. $\dfrac{3}{5}$

C. $\dfrac{4}{5}$

D. $\dfrac{4}{3}$

E. $\dfrac{5}{3}$

SSAT UPPER LEVEL Math
Practice Test 2

Section 1

25 questions

Total time for this section: 30 Minutes

You may NOT use a calculator for this test.

1) If $x - 10 = -10$, then $x \times 3 = ?$

$x = 0$

A. 10

B. 30

C. 60

D. 90

E. 0

2) Mia plans to buy a bracelet for every one of her 16 friends for their party. There are three bracelet in each packs. How many packs must she buy?

A. 3

B. 4

C. 5

D. 6

E. 10

3) If Logan ran 2.5 miles in half an hour, his average speed was?

A. 1.25 miles per hour

B. 2.5 miles per hour

C. 3.75 miles per hour

D. 5 miles per hour

E. 10 miles per hour

4) What is the value of the "4" in number 131.493?

   A. 4 ones
   B. 4 tenths
   C. 4 hundredths
   D. 4 tens
   E. 4 thousandths

5) 0.03 × 12.00 =?

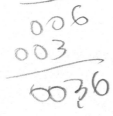

   A. 3.6
   B. 36.00
   C. 0.36
   D. 3.06
   E. 0.036

6) The distance between cities A and B is approximately 2,600 miles. If Alice drives an average of 68 miles per hour, how many hours will it take Alice to drive from city A to city B?

   A. Approximately 41 hours
   B. Approximately 38 hours
   C. Approximately 29 hours
   D. Approximately 27 hours
   E. Approximately 21 hours

7) In a classroom of 60 students, 42 are female. What percentage of the class is male?

A. 34%

B. 22%

C. 30%

D. 26%

E. 15%

8) An employee's rating on performance appraisals for the last three quarters were 92, 88 and 86. If the required yearly average to qualify for the promotion is 90, what rating should the fourth quarter be?

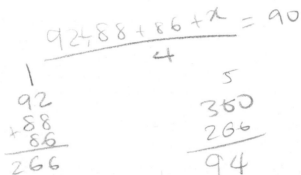

A. 91

B. 92

C. 93

D. 94

E. 95

9) Given the diagram, what is the perimeter of the quadrilateral?

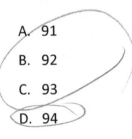

A. 54

B. 66

C. 620

D. 16740

E. 33480

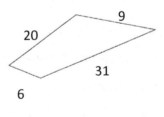

10) A pizza maker has x pounds of flour to make pizzas. After he has used 55 pounds of flour, how much flour is left? The expression that correctly represents the quantity of flour left is:

A. $55 + x$

B. $\dfrac{55}{x}$

C. $55 - x$

D. $x - 55$

E. $55x$

11) A steak dinner at a restaurant costs $8.25. If a man buys a steak dinner for himself and 3 friends, what will the total cost be?

A. $33

B. $17.01

C. $27

D. $21.5

E. 11

12) What is the slope of the line that is perpendicular to the line with equation $7x + y = 12$?

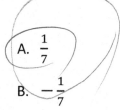

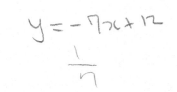

A. $\dfrac{1}{7}$

B. $-\dfrac{1}{7}$

C. $\dfrac{7}{12}$

D. 7

E. -7

13) A cruise line ship left Port A and traveled 50 miles due west and then 120 miles due north. At this point, what is the shortest distance from the cruise to port A?

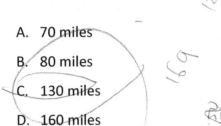

   A. 70 miles

   B. 80 miles

   C. 130 miles

   D. 160 miles

   E. 170 miles

14) Last week 24,000 fans attended a football match. This week three times as many bought tickets, but one sixth of them cancelled their tickets. How many are attending this week?

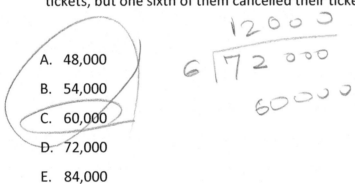

   A. 48,000

   B. 54,000

   C. 60,000

   D. 72,000

   E. 84,000

15) Two third of 18 is equal to $\frac{2}{5}$ of what number?

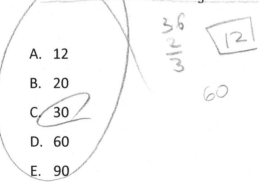

   A. 12

   B. 20

   C. 30

   D. 60

   E. 90

16) In 1999, the average worker's income increased $2,000 per year starting from $24,000 annual salary. Which equation represents income greater than average? (I = income, x = number of years after 1999)

A. $I > 2000\,x + 24000$

B. $I > -2000\,x + 24000$

C. $I < -2000\,x + 24000$

D. $I < 2000\,x - 24000$

E. $I < 24,000\,x + 24000$

Questions 17 to 19 are based on the following data

The result of a research shows the number of men and women in four cities of a country.

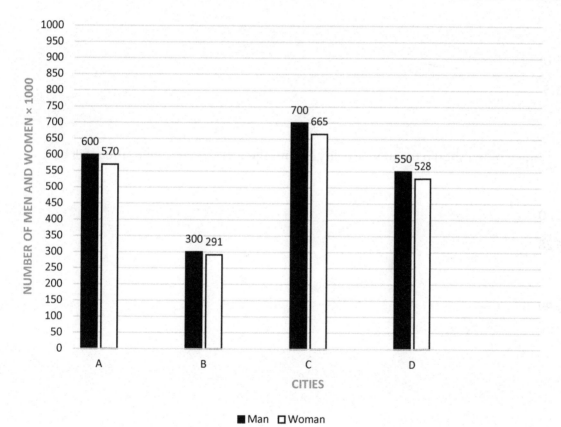

17) What's the maximum ratio of woman to man in the four cities?

   A. 0.98

   B. 0.97

   C. 0.96

   D. 0.95

   E. 0.93

18) What's the ratio of percentage of men in city A to percentage of women in city C?

   A. 0.9

   B. 0.95

   C. 1

   D. 1.05

   E. 1.5

19) How many women should be added to city D until the ratio of women to men will be 1.2?

   A. 120

   B. 128

   C. 132

   D. 160

   E. 165

20) In the figure, MN is 40 cm. How long is ON?

A. 25 cm

B. 20 cm

C. 15 cm

D. 10 cm

E. 5 cm

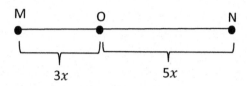

21) $\sqrt[5]{x^{16}} = ?$

A. $x^3 \sqrt[5]{x}$

B. $80x$

C. x^{11}

D. x^{80}

E. x^4

22) What is the difference of smallest 4–digit number and biggest 4–digit number?

A. 6666

B. 6789

C. 8888

D. 8999

E. 9999

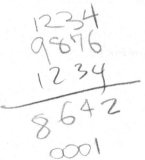

23) Rectangle A has a length of 8 cm and a width of 4cm, and rectangle B has a length of 5 cm and a width of 4 cm, what is the percent of ratio of the perimeter of rectangle B to rectangle A?

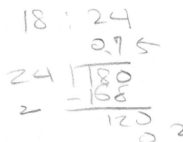

A. 15%

B. 25%

C. 50%

D. 75%

E. 133.3%

24) John traveled 150 km in 6 hours and Alice traveled 180 km in 4 hours. What is the ratio of the average speed of John to average speed of Alice?

A. $3:2$

B. $2:3$

C. $5:9$

D. $5:6$

E. $11:16$

25) Solve the following equation for y?

$$\frac{x}{2+3} = \frac{y}{10-7}$$

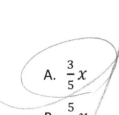

A. $\frac{3}{5}x$

B. $\frac{5}{3}x$

C. $3x$

D. $2x$

E. $\frac{1}{2}x$

SSAT UPPER LEVEL Math
Practice Test 2

Section 2

25 questions

Total time for this section: 30 Minutes

You may NOT use a calculator for this test.

1) Which of the following is a whole number ?

    A. $\frac{2}{3} \times \frac{9}{5}$

    B. $\frac{1}{2} + \frac{1}{4}$

    C. $\frac{21}{6}$

    D. $2.5 + 1$

    E. $2.5 + \frac{7}{2}$

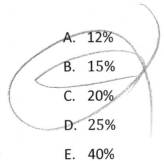

2) Sophia purchased a sofa for $530.40. The sofa is regularly priced at $624. What was the percent discount Sophia received on the sofa?

    A. 12%

    B. 15%

    C. 20%

    D. 25%

    E. 40%

3) If $\frac{2}{5}$ of a number equal to 12 then $\frac{2}{3}$ of the same number is:

    A. 48

    B. 45

    C. 30

    D. 24

    E. 20

4) $0.42 \times 11.8 = ?$

A. 4.956

B. 4.965

C. 5.956

D. 5.965

E. 5.695

5) $5\frac{3}{7} \times 4\frac{1}{5} = ?$

A. $23\frac{1}{5}$

B. $23\frac{4}{5}$

C. $22\frac{4}{5}$

D. $22\frac{1}{5}$

E. 21

6) A swimming pool holds 2,000 cubic feet of water. The swimming pool is 25 feet long and 10 feet wide. How deep is the swimming pool?

A. 2 feet

B. 4 feet

C. 6 feet

D. 7 feet

E. 8 feet

7) In the figure below, line A is parallel to line B. What is the value of angle x?

A. 35 degree

B. 45 degree

C. 90 degree

D. 100 degree

E. 145 degree

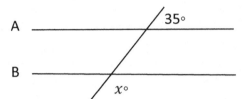

8) We can put 24 colored pencils in each box and we have 408 colored pencils. How many boxes do we need?

A. 13

B. 14

C. 15

D. 16

E. 17

9) A bank is offering 3.5% simple interest on a savings account. If you deposit $12,000, how much interest will you earn in two years?

A. $420

B. $840

C. $4,200

D. $8,400

E. $9,000

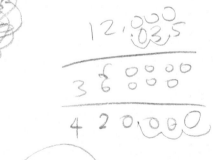

10) How long does a 420–miles trip take moving at 50 miles per hour (mph)?

   A. 6 hours

   B. 6 hours and 24 minutes

   C. 8 hours and 24 minutes

   D. 8 hours and 30 minutes

   E. 10 hours and 30 minutes

11) 7 cubed is the same as:

   A. 7×7

   B. 7×7×7×7

   C. 14

   D. 343

   E. 16807

12) If car A drives 600 miles in 8 hours and car B drives the same distance in 7.5 hours, how many miles per hour does car B drive faster than car A?

   A. 80

   B. 75

   C. 15

   D. 10

   E. 5

13) The ratio of boys to girls in a school is 2:3. If there are 600 students in a school, how many boys are in the school?

120

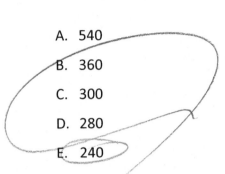

A. 540

B. 360

C. 300

D. 280

E. 240

14) When a number is subtracted from 24 and the difference is divided by that number, the result is 3. What is the value of the number?

A. 2

B. 4

C. 6

D. 12

E. 24

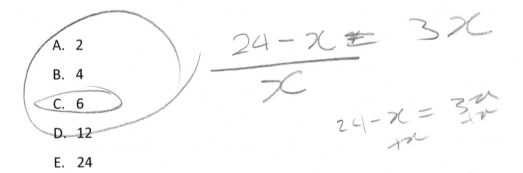

$$\frac{24 - x = 3x}{x}$$

$$24 - x = 3x$$
$$+x \qquad +x$$

15) A construction company is building a wall. The company can build 30 cm of the wall per minute. After 40 minutes construction, $\frac{3}{4}$ of the wall is completed. How high is the wall?

A. 9 m

B. 12 m

C. 16 m

D. 18 m

E. 20 m

30
40
1200

16) $\frac{(7+5)^2}{4} + 5 = ?$

A. 41

B. 42

C. 43

D. 44

E. 45

17) If $y = 4ab + 3b^3$, what is y when $a = 2$ and $b = 3$?

A. 24

B. 31

C. 36

D. 51

E. 105

18) Which of the following shows the numbers in increasing order?

A. $\frac{2}{3}, \frac{5}{7}, \frac{8}{11}, \frac{3}{4}$

B. $\frac{5}{7}, \frac{3}{4}, \frac{8}{11}, \frac{2}{3}$

C. $\frac{8}{11}, \frac{3}{4}, \frac{5}{7}, \frac{2}{3}$

D. $\frac{5}{7}, \frac{8}{11}, \frac{3}{4}, \frac{2}{3}$

E. None of the above

19) The area of a circle is 64 π. What is the circumference of the circle?

   A. 8 π

   B. 12 π

   C. 16 π

   D. 32 π

   E. 64 π

20) A company pays its employee $7000 plus 2% of all sales profit. If x is the number of all sales profit, which of the following represents the employee's revenue?

   A. $0.02x$

   B. $0.98x - 7000$

   C. $0.02x + 7000$

   D. $0.98x + 7000$

   E. $0.09x$

21) If 60% of x equal to 30% of 20, then what is the value of $(x + 5)^2$?

   A. 25.25

   B. 26

   C. 26.01

   D. 225

   E. 11,025

22) What is the greatest common factor of 36 and 54?

    A. 28

    B. 24

    C. 18

    D. 12

    E. 8

23) Find $\frac{1}{4}$ of $\frac{2}{5}$ of 120?

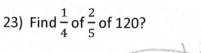

    A. 16

    B. 12

    C. 8

    D. 4

    E. 2

24) If the interior angles of a quadrilateral are in the ratio 1:2:2:5, what is the measure of the largest angle?

    A. 36°

    B. 72°

    C. 108°

    D. 144°

    E. 180°

25) The length of a rectangle is $\frac{5}{4}$ times its width. If the width is 16, what is the perimeter of this rectangle?

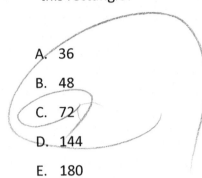

A. 36

B. 48

C. 72

D. 144

E. 180

SSAT UPPER LEVEL Math Practice Tests Answers and Explanations

SSAT Mathematics Practice Test 1						
Section 1				**Section 2**		
1-	D	14-	B	1-	B	14-	D
2-	D	15-	C	2-	C	15-	D
3-	C	16-	B	3-	A	16-	D
4-	A	17-	B	4-	A	17-	E
5-	C	18-	C	5-	C	18-	A
6-	E	19-	B	6-	B	19-	E
7-	E	20-	B	7-	E	20-	B
8-	D	21-	B	8-	E	21-	B
9-	A	22-	D	9-	E	22-	C
10-	A	23-	B	10-	C	23-	C
11-	B	24-	D	11-	B	24-	D
12-	A	25-	D	12-	D	25-	E
13-	D			13-	E		

SSAT Mathematics Practice Test 2

Section 1				Section 2			
1-	E	14-	C	1-	E	14-	C
2-	D	15-	C	2-	B	15-	C
3-	D	16-	A	3-	B	16-	A
4-	B	17-	B	4-	A	17-	E
5-	C	18-	D	5-	C	18-	A
6-	B	19-	C	6-	E	19-	C
7-	C	20-	A	7-	E	20-	C
8-	D	21-	A	8-	E	21-	D
9-	B	22-	D	9-	B	22-	C
10-	D	23-	D	10-	C	23-	B
11-	A	24-	C	11-	D	24-	E
12-	A	25-	A	12-	E	25-	C
13-	C			13-	E		

Score Your Test

SSAT scores are broken down by its three sections: Verbal, Quantitative (or Math), and Reading. A sum of the three sections is also reported.

For the Upper Level SSAT, the score range is 500-800, the lowest possible score a student can earn is 500 and the highest score is 800 for each section. A student receives 1 point for every correct answer and loses $\frac{1}{4}$ point for each incorrect answer. No points are lost by skipping a question.

The total scaled score for an Upper Level SSAT is the sum of the scores for the quantitative, verbal, and reading sections. A student will also receive a percentile score of between 1-99% that compares that student's test scores with those of other test takers of same grade and gender from the past 3 years.

Use the following table to convert SSAT Upper level raw score to scaled score.

SSAT Upper Level Math Scaled Scores	
Raw Scores	Mathematics
50	800
45	790
40	765
35	740
30	715
25	694
20	668
15	642
10	605
5	575
0	544
-5	512
- 10 and lower	500

SSAT UPPER LEVEL Math Practice Tests Explanations

SSAT UPPER LEVEL Math Practice Test 1

Section 1

1) Choice D is correct

$$\frac{25}{A} + 1 = 6 \rightarrow \frac{25}{A} = 6 - 1 = 5$$

$$\rightarrow 25 = 5A \rightarrow A = \frac{25}{5} = 5$$

$$25 + A = 25 + 5 = 30$$

2) Choice D is correct

Number of packs equal to: $\frac{20}{3} \cong 6.677$

Therefore, the school must purchase 7 packs.

3) Choice C is correct

The area of the floor is: 6 cm × 24 cm = 144 cm^2

The number of tiles needed = 144 ÷ 8 = 18

4) Choice A is correct

Number of rotates in 12 second equal to: $\frac{300 \times 12}{8} = 450$

5) Choice C is correct

    A. Number of books sold in April is: 380

        Number of books sold in July is: 760 $\rightarrow \frac{380}{760} = \frac{38}{76} = \frac{1}{2}$

    B. number of books sold in July is: 760

        Half the number of books sold in May is: $\frac{1140}{2} = 570 \rightarrow 760 > 570$

    C. number of books sold in June is: 190

        Half the number of books sold in April is: $\frac{380}{2} = 190 \rightarrow 190 = 190$

    D. $380 + 190 = 570 < 760$

    E. $380 < 760$

6) Choice E is correct

The digit in tens place is 1.

The digit in the thousandths place is 4.

Therefore; $1 + 4 = 5$

7) Choice E is correct

The amount of money that Jack earns for one hour: $\frac{\$616}{44} = \$14$

Number of additional hours that he need to work in order to make enough money is:

$$\frac{\$826 - \$616}{1.5 \times \$14} = 10$$

Number of total hours is: $44 + 10 = 54$

8) Choice D is correct

$$12.124 \div 0.002 = \frac{\frac{12,124}{1,000}}{\frac{2}{1,000}} = \frac{12,124}{2} = 6,062$$

9) Choice A is correct

$$\frac{1\frac{3}{4} + \frac{1}{3}}{2\frac{1}{2} - \frac{15}{8}} = \frac{\frac{7}{4} + \frac{1}{3}}{\frac{5}{2} - \frac{15}{8}} = \frac{\frac{21+4}{12}}{\frac{20-15}{8}} = \frac{\frac{25}{12}}{\frac{5}{8}} = \frac{25 \times 8}{12 \times 5} = \frac{5 \times 2}{3 \times 1} = \frac{10}{3} \cong 3.33$$

10) Choice A is correct

First, find the number.

Let x be the number. Write the equation and solve for x.

150 % of a number is 75, then:

$1.5 \times x = 75 \rightarrow x = 75 \div 1.5 = 50$

90 % of 50 is:

$0.9 \times 50 = 45$

11) Choice B is correct

$5 \blacksquare 11 = \sqrt{5^2 + 11} = \sqrt{25 + 11} = \sqrt{36} = 6$

12) Choice A is correct

Let x be the capacity of one tank. Then, $\frac{2}{5}x = 200 \rightarrow x = \frac{200 \times 5}{2} = 500$ Liters

The amount of water in three tanks is equal to: $3 \times 500 = 1500$ Liters

13) Choice D is correct

Let q be the quotient of 7.5 and 0.15 then: $q = \frac{7.5}{0.15} = \frac{\frac{75}{10}}{\frac{15}{100}} = \frac{75 \times 100}{15 \times 10} = \frac{75}{15} \times \frac{100}{10} = 5 \times 10 = 50$

14) Choice B is correct

Average $= \frac{\text{sum of terms}}{\text{number of terms}}$

The sum of the weight of all girls is: $18 \times 60 = 1080$ kg

The sum of the weight of all boys is: $32 \times 62 = 1984$ kg

The sum of the weight of all students is: $1080 + 1984 = 3064$ kg

Average $= \frac{3064}{50} = 61.28$

15) Choice C is correct

$1 < x < 4 \rightarrow 2 \times 1 < 2 \times x < 2 \times 4 \rightarrow 2 < 2x < 8$

$\rightarrow 2 + 1 < 2x + 1 < 8 + 1 \rightarrow 3 < 2x + 1 < 8$

Minimum value of $2x + 1$ is 3

16) Choice B is correct

$x = 20 + 125 = 145$

17) Choice B is correct

Let b be the amount of time Alec can do the job, then,

$\frac{1}{a} + \frac{1}{b} = \frac{1}{100} \rightarrow \frac{1}{300} + \frac{1}{b} = \frac{1}{100} \rightarrow \frac{1}{b} = \frac{1}{100} - \frac{1}{300} = \frac{2}{300} = \frac{1}{150}$

Then: $b = 150$ minutes

18) Choice C is correct

The smallest number is -15. To find the largest possible value of one of the other five integers, we need to choose the smallest possible integers for four of them. Let x be the largest number. Then:

$$-70 = (-15) + (-14) + (-13) + (-12) + (-11) + x \rightarrow -70 = -65 + x$$

$$\rightarrow x = -70 + 65 = -5$$

19) Choice B is correct

Let's review the options provided.

  A. 4. In 4 years, David will be 46 and Ava will be 10. 46 is not 4 times 10.
  B. 6. In 6 years, David will be 48 and Ava will be 12. 48 is 4 times 12!
  C. 8. In 8 years, David will be 80 and Ava will be 14. 50 is not 4 times 14.
  D. 10. In 10 years, David will be 52 and Ava will be 16. 52 is not 4 times 16.
  E. 14. In 14 years, David will be 56 and Ava will be 20. 56 is not 4 times 20.

20) Choice B is correct

Let x be the cost of one-kilogram orange, then: $\quad 3x + (2 \times 4.2) = 26.4 \rightarrow 3x + 8.4 =$
$26.4 \rightarrow 3x = 26.4 - 8.4 \rightarrow 3x = 18 \rightarrow x = \frac{18}{3} = \$6$

21) Choice B is correct

The equation of a line in slope intercept form is: $y = \text{m}x + b$

Solve for y.

$$4x - 2y = 12 \Rightarrow -2y = 12 - 4x \Rightarrow y = (12 - 4x) \div (-2) \Rightarrow$$

$$y = 2x - 6$$

The slope is 2

The slope of the line perpendicular to this line is:

$$m_1 \times m_2 = -1 \Rightarrow 2 \times m_2 = -1 \Rightarrow m_2 = -\frac{1}{2}$$

22) *Choice D is correct*

Use the information provided in the question to draw the shape.

Use Pythagorean Theorem: $a^2 + b^2 = c^2$

$80^2 + 150^2 = c^2 \Rightarrow 6400 + 22500 = c^2 \Rightarrow 28900 = c^2 \Rightarrow c = 170$

1500 miles

Port A

80 miles

23) *Choice B is correct*

Choices A, C and D are incorrect because 80% of each of the numbers is non-whole number.

F.	49,	$80\% \ of \ 49 \ = \ 0.80 \times 49 = 39.2$
G.	35,	$80\% \ of \ 35 = 0.80 \times 35 = 28$
H.	12,	$80\% \ of \ 12 = 0.80 \times 12 = 9.6$
I.	32,	$80\% \ of \ 32 = 0.80 \times 32 = 25.6$
J.	16,	$80\% \ of \ 16 = 0.80 \times 16 = 12.8$

24) *Choice D is correct*

If the length of the box is 27, then the width of the box is one third of it, 9, and the height of the box is 3 (one third of the width). The volume of the box is:

V = lwh = (27) (9) (3) = 729

25) *Choice D is correct*

The amount of money for x bookshelf is: $\quad 100x$

Then, the total cost of all bookshelves is equal to: $\quad 100x + 800$

The total cost, in dollar, per bookshelf is: $\dfrac{Total\ cost}{number\ of\ items} = \dfrac{100x+800}{x}$

SSAT UPPER LEVEL Math Practice Tests Explanations

SSAT UPPER LEVEL Math Practice Test 1

Section 2

1) Choice B is correct

$\frac{17+11}{2} = \frac{28}{2} = 14$ Then, $14 - 11 = 3$

2) Choice C is correct

$\frac{91501}{305} \cong 300.0032 \cong 300$

3) Choice E is correct

Grade of Alex = $16 - k$

4) Choice A is correct

The Area that one liter of paint is required: $72cm \times 100cm = 7200cm^2$

Remember: $1 \ m^2 = 10,000 \ cm^2 \ (100 \times 100 = 10,000)$, then, $7200cm^2 = 0.72 \ m^2$

Amount of liters of paint we need: $\frac{36}{0.72} = 50$ liters

5) Choice C is correct

Let's review the options provided:

A. $x = 2 \rightarrow$ The perimeter of the figure is: $2 + 4 + 2 + 2 + 2 = 12 \neq 20$
B. $x = 3 \rightarrow$ The perimeter of the figure is: $2 + 4 + 2 + 3 + 3 = 14 \neq 20$
C. $x = 6 \rightarrow$ The perimeter of the figure is: $2 + 4 + 2 + 6 + 6 = 20 = 20$
D. $x = 9 \rightarrow$ The perimeter of the figure is: $2 + 4 + 2 + 9 + 9 = 26 \neq 20$
E. $x = 12 \rightarrow$ The perimeter of the figure is: $2 + 4 + 2 + 12 + 12 = 32 \neq 20$

6) Choice B is correct

$$750 - 7\frac{7}{15} = 750 - \frac{(7 \times 15) + 7}{15} = 750 - \frac{112}{15} = \frac{(750 \times 15) - 112}{15} = \frac{11138}{15} = 742\frac{8}{15}$$

7) Choice E is correct

Let's review the options provided:

A. $10 \times \frac{1}{2} = \frac{10}{2} = 5 = 5$
B. $25 \times \frac{1}{5} = \frac{25}{5} = 5 = 5$
C. $2 \times \frac{5}{2} = \frac{10}{2} = 5 = 5$
D. $6 \times \frac{5}{6} = \frac{30}{6} = 5 = 5$
E. $5 \times \frac{1}{5} = \frac{5}{5} = 1 \neq 5$

8) Choice E is correct

Find the difference of each pairs of numbers:

2, 3, 5, 8, 12, 17, 23, ___, 38

The difference of 2 and 3 is 1, 3 and 5 is 2, 5 and 8 is 3, 8 and 12 is 4, 12 and 17 is 5, 17 and 23 is 6, 23 and next number should be 7. The number is 23 + 7 = 30

9) Choice E is correct

Number of times that driver rest $= \frac{20}{4} = 5$

Driver's rest time $= 1$ hour and 12 minutes $= 72$ minutes

Then, 5×72 minutes $= 360$ minutes

1 hour $= 60$ minutes $\rightarrow 360$ minutes $= 6$ hours

10) Choice C is correct

Let x be the original price.

If the price of the sofa is decreased by 25% to \$420, then: 75 % of $x = 420 \Rightarrow 0.75x = 420 \Rightarrow x = 420 \div 0.75 = 560$

11) Choice B is correct

Number of Mathematics book: $0.3 \times 840 = 252$
Number of English book: $0.15 \times 840 = 126$
Product of number of Mathematics and number of English book: $252 \times 126 = 31752$

12) Choice D is correct

The angle α is: $0.3 \times 360 = 108°$
The angle β is: $0.15 \times 360 = 54°$

13) Choice E is correct

$3y + 5 < 29 \rightarrow 3y < 29 - 5 \rightarrow 3y < 24 \rightarrow y < 8$

14) *Choice D is correct*

The capacity of a red box is 20% bigger than the capacity of a blue box and it can hold 30 books.

Therefore, we want to find a number that 20% bigger than that number is 30. Let x be that

number. Then: $\qquad 1.20 \times x = 30$, Divide both sides of the equation by 1.2. Then:

$$x = \frac{30}{1.20} = 25$$

15) *Choice D is correct*

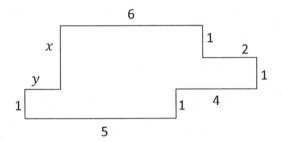

$x + 1 = 1 + 1 + 1 \rightarrow x = 2$

$y + 6 + 2 = 5 + 4 \rightarrow y + 8 = 9 \rightarrow y = 1$

Then, the perimeter is:

$1 + 5 + 1 + 4 + 1 + 2 + 1 + 6 + 2 + 1 = 24$

16) *Choice D is correct*

Amount of available petrol in tank: $50.2 - 5.28 - 25.9 + 10.31 = 28.79$ liters

17) *Choice E is correct*

We have two equations and three unknown variables, therefore x cannot be obtained.

18) *Choice A is correct*

Perimeter of figure A is: $2\pi r = 2\pi \frac{16}{2} = 16\pi = 16 \times 3 = 48$

Area of figure B is: $5 \times 12 = 60$

Average $= \frac{48 + 60}{2} = \frac{108}{2} = 54$

19) *Choice E is correct*

Let put some values for a and b. If $a = 9$ and $b = 2 \rightarrow a \times b = 18 \rightarrow \frac{18}{3} = 6 \rightarrow 18$ is divisible
by 3 then;

    A. $a + b = 9 + 2 = 11$ is not divisible by 3
    B. $3a - b = (3 \times 9) - 2 = 27 - 2 = 25$ is not divisible by 3

If $a = 11$ and $b = 3 \rightarrow a \times b = 33 \rightarrow \frac{33}{3} = 11$ is divisible by 3 then;

    C. $a - 3b = 11 - (3 \times 3) = 11 - 9 = 2$ is not divisible by 3

D. $\frac{a}{b} = \frac{11}{3}$ is not divisible by 3

20)   *Choice B is correct*

Since, E is the midpoint of AB, then the area of all triangles DAE, DEF, CFE and CBE are equal.

Let x be the area of one of the triangle, then: $4x = 100 \rightarrow x = 25$

The area of DEC $= 2x = 2(25) = 50$

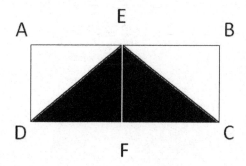

21)   *Choice B is correct*

The angles on a straight line add up to 180 degrees. Then:

F. $y = 15 \rightarrow x + 25 + y + 2x + y = 35 + 25 + 15 + 2(35) + 15 = 160 \neq 180$
G. $y = 25 \rightarrow x + 25 + y + 2x + y = 35 + 25 + 25 + 2(35) + 25 = 180$
H. $y = 35 \rightarrow x + 25 + y + 2x + y = 35 + 25 + 35 + 2(35) + 35 = 200 \neq 180$
I. $y = 45 \rightarrow x + 25 + y + 2x + y = 35 + 25 + 45 + 2(35) + 45 = 220 \neq 180$
J. $y = 55 \rightarrow x + 25 + y + 2x + y = 35 + 25 + 55 + 2(35) + 55 = 240 \neq 180$

22)   *Choice C is correct*

Set of numbers that are not composite between 1 and 25: A= {2, 3, 5, 7, 11, 13, 17, 19, 23}

$$\text{Probability} = \frac{number\ of\ desired\ outcomes}{number\ of\ total\ outcomes} = \frac{9}{25}$$

23)   *Choice C is correct*

$$712 \div 3 = \frac{712}{3} = \frac{700 + 10 + 2}{3} = \frac{700}{3} + \frac{10}{3} + \frac{2}{3}$$

24)   *Choice D is correct*

$$\frac{2}{5} \times 25 = \frac{50}{5} = 10$$

25) *Choice E is correct*

A. $x = \frac{1}{2} \to \frac{5}{9} + \frac{1}{2} = \frac{10+}{18} = \frac{19}{18} \cong 1.056 < 2$

B. $x = \frac{3}{5} \to \frac{5}{9} + \frac{3}{5} = \frac{25+27}{45} = \frac{52}{45} \cong 1.16 < 2$

C. $x = \frac{4}{5} \to \frac{5}{9} + \frac{4}{5} = \frac{25+}{45} = \frac{61}{45} \cong 1.36 < 2$

D. $x = \frac{4}{3} \to \frac{5}{9} + \frac{4}{3} = \frac{5+12}{9} = \frac{17}{9} \cong 1.89 < 2$

E. $x = \frac{5}{3} \to \frac{5}{9} + \frac{5}{3} = \frac{5+15}{9} = \frac{20}{9} \cong 2.2 > 2$

SSAT UPPER LEVEL Math Practice Tests Explanations

SSAT UPPER LEVEL Math Practice Test 2

Section 1

1) Choice E is correct

$x - 10 = -10 \rightarrow x = -10 + 10 \rightarrow x = 0$

Then; $x \times 3 = 0 \times 3 = 0$

2) Choice D is correct

Number of packs needed equals to: $\frac{16}{3} \cong 5.33$

Then school must purchase 6 packs.

3) Choice D is correct

His average speed was: $\frac{2.5}{0.5} = 5$ miles per hour

4) Choice B is correct

Digit 4 is in the tenths place.

5) Choice C is correct

$$0.03 \times 12.00 = \frac{3}{100} \times \frac{12}{1} = \frac{36}{100} = 0.36$$

6) Choice B is correct

The time it takes to drive from city A to city B is: $\frac{2600}{68} = 38.23$

It's approximately 38 hours.

7) Choice C is correct

Number of males in classroom is: $60 - 42 = 18$

Then, the percentage of males in the classroom is: $\frac{18}{60} \times 100 = 0.3 \times 100 = 30\%$

8) Choice D is correct

Let x be fourth quarter rating, therefore; $\frac{92+38+86+x}{4} = 90$

Multiply both sides of the above equation by 4. Then:

$$4 \times \left(\frac{92 + 38 + 86 + x}{4}\right) = 4 \times 90 \rightarrow 92 + 88 + 86 + x = 360 \rightarrow 266 + x = 360 \rightarrow x$$
$$= 360 - 266 = 94$$

9) *Choice B is correct*

The perimeter of the quadrilateral is: $6 + 20 + 9 + 31 = 66$

10) *Choice D is correct*

The amount of flour is: $x - 55$

11) *Choice A is correct*

For one person the total cost is: $8.25

Therefore, for four persons, the total cost is: $4 \times \$8.25 = \$33$

12) *Choice A is correct*

The equation of a line in slope intercept form is: $y = \mathrm{m}x + b$

Solve for y.

$7x + y = 12 \Rightarrow y = -7x + 12$

$y = -7x + 12$

The slope of this line is -7.

The slope of the line perpendicular to this line is:

$m_1 \times m_2 = -1 \Rightarrow -7 \times m_2 = -1 \Rightarrow m_2 = \frac{1}{7}$

13) *Choice C is correct*

Use the information provided in the question to draw the shape.

Use Pythagorean Theorem: $a^2 + b^2 = c^2$

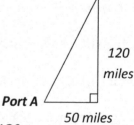

$50^2 + 120^2 = c^2 \Rightarrow 2500 + 14400 = c^2 \Rightarrow 16900 = c^2 \Rightarrow c = 130$

14) *Choice C is correct*

Three times of 24,000 is 72,000. One sixth of them cancelled their tickets.

One sixth of 72,000 equals 12,000 ($1/6 \times 72000 = 12000$).

60,000 ($72000 - 12000 = 60000$) fans are attending this week

15) *Choice C is correct*

Let x be the number. Write the equation and solve for x.

$\frac{2}{3} \times 18 = \frac{2}{5}x \rightarrow \frac{2\times18}{3} = \frac{2x}{5}$, use cross multiplication to solve for x.

$5 \times 36 = 2x \times 3 \Rightarrow 180 = 6x \Rightarrow x = 30$

16) *Choice A is correct*

Let x be the number of years. Therefore, $2,000 per year equals $2000x$.

Starting from $24,000 annual salary means you should add that amount to $2000x$.

Income more than that is:

$I > 2000\ x\ +\ 24000$

17) *Choice B is correct*

Ratio of women to men in city A: $\frac{570}{600}$=0.95

Ratio of women to men in city B: $\frac{291}{300}$=0.97

Ratio of women to men in city C: $\frac{665}{700}$=0.95

Ratio of women to men in city D: $\frac{528}{550}$=0.96

0.97 is the maximum ratio of woman to man in the four cities.

18) *Choice D is correct*

Percentage of men in city A $= \frac{600}{1170} \times 100 = 51.28\%$

Percentage of women in city C $= \frac{665}{1365} \times 100 = 48.72\%$

Percentage of men in city A to percentage of women in city C $= \frac{51.28}{48.72} = 1.05$

19) *Choice C is correct*

Let the number of women should be added to city D be x, then:

$\frac{528 + x}{550} = 1.2 \rightarrow 528 + x = 550 \times 1.2 = 660 \rightarrow x = 132$

20) *Choice A is correct*

The length of MN is equal to: $3x + 5x = 8x$

Then: $8x = 40 \rightarrow x = \frac{40}{8} = 5$

The length of ON is equal to: $5x = 5 \times 5 = 25$ cm

21) *Choice A is correct*

$$\sqrt[5]{x^{16}} = \sqrt[5]{x^{15} \times x} = \sqrt[5]{x^{15}} \times \sqrt[5]{x} = x^{\frac{15}{5}} \times \sqrt[5]{x} = x^3 \sqrt[5]{x}$$

22) *Choice D is correct*

Smallest 4–digit number is 1000, and biggest 4–digit number is 9999. The difference is: 8999

23) *Choice D is correct*

Perimeter of rectangle A is equal to: $2 \times (8 + 4) = 2 \times 12 = 24$

Perimeter of rectangle A is equal to: $2 \times (5 + 4) = 2 \times 9 = 18$

Therefore: $\frac{18}{24} \times 100 = 0.75 \times 100 = 75\%$

24) *Choice C is correct*

The average speed of John is: $150 \div 6 = 25$ km

The average speed of Alice is: $180 \div 4 = 45$ km

Write the ratio and simplify.

$25 : 45 \Rightarrow 5 : 9$

25) *Choice A is correct*

$$\frac{x}{2+3} = \frac{y}{10-7} \rightarrow \frac{x}{5} = \frac{y}{3} \rightarrow 5y = 3x \rightarrow y = \frac{3}{5}x$$

SSAT UPPER LEVEL Math Practice Tests Explanations

SSAT UPPER LEVEL Math Practice Test 2

Section 2

1) Choice E is correct

F. $\frac{2}{3} \times \frac{9}{5} = \frac{6}{5}$ is not equal to whole number

G. $\frac{1}{2} + \frac{1}{4} = \frac{2+1}{4} = \frac{3}{4}$ is not equal to whole number

H. $\frac{21}{6} = \frac{7}{2} = 3.5$ is not equal to whole number

I. $2.5 + 1 = 3.5$ is not equal to whole number

J. $2.5 + \frac{7}{2} = 2.5 + 3.5 = 6$ is equal to whole number

2) Choice B is correct

The question is this: 530.40 is what percent of 624?

Use percent formula:

$$Part = \frac{percent}{100} \times whole$$

$$530.40 = \frac{percent}{100} \times 624 \rightarrow 530.40 = \frac{percent \times 624}{100} \rightarrow 53040 = percent \times 624$$

Then, Percent $= \frac{53040}{624} = 85$

530.40 is 85 % of 624. Therefore, the discount is: 100% − 85% = 15%

3) Choice B is correct

Let x be the number, then; $\quad \frac{2}{5}x = 12 \rightarrow x = \frac{5 \times 12}{2} = 30$

Therefore: $\quad \frac{2}{3}x = \frac{2}{3} \times 30 = 20$

4) Choice A is correct

$$0.42 \times 11.8 = \frac{42}{100} \times \frac{118}{10} = \frac{42 \times 118}{100 \times 10} = \frac{4956}{1000} = 4.956$$

5) Choice C is correct

$$5\frac{3}{7} \times 4\frac{1}{5} = \frac{38}{7} \times \frac{21}{5} = \frac{38 \times 21}{7 \times 5} = \frac{798}{35} = \frac{114}{5} = 22\frac{4}{5}$$

6) Choice E is correct

Use formula of rectangle prism volume.

V = (length) (width) (height) ⇒ 2000 = (25) (10) (height) ⇒ height = 2000 ÷ 250 = 8

7) *Choice E is correct*

The angle x and 35 are complementary angles. Therefore:

$x + 35 = 180$

$180° - 35° = 145°$

8) *Choice E is correct*

Number of boxes equal to: $\frac{408}{24} = \frac{102}{6} = \frac{34}{2} = 17$

9) *Choice B is correct*

Use simple interest formula:

$I = prt$

(I = interest, p = principal, r = rate, t = time)

$I = (12000)(0.035)(2) = \$840$

10) *Choice C is correct*

Use distance formula:

Distance = Rate × time ⟹ 420 = 50 × T, divide both sides by 50. 420 / 50 = T ⟹ T = 8.4 hours.

Change hours to minutes for the decimal part. 0.4 hours = 0.4 × 60 = 24 minutes

11) *Choice D is correct*

7 cubed is: $7 \times 7 \times 7 = 49 \times 7 = 343$

12) *Choice E is correct*

Speed of car A is: $\frac{600}{8} = 75$ Km/h

Speed of car B is: $\frac{600}{7.5} = 80$ Km/h

→ 80 − 75 = 5 Km/h

13) *Choice E is correct*

The ratio of boys to girls is 2:3. Therefore, there are 2 boys out of 5 students. To find the answer, first divide the total number of students by 5, then multiply the result by 2.

600 ÷ 5 = 120 ⟹ 120 × 2 = 240

14)   *Choice C is correct*

Let's review the options provided:

A. $24 - 2 = 22 \to \frac{22}{2} = 11 \neq 3$

B. $24 - 4 = 20 \to \frac{20}{4} = 5 \neq 3$

C. $24 - 6 = 18 \to \frac{18}{6} = 3 = 3$

D. $24 - 12 = 12 \to \frac{12}{12} = 1 \neq 3$

E. $24 - 24 = 0 \to \frac{0}{24} = 0 \neq 3$

15)   *Choice C is correct*

The rate of construction company $= \frac{30 \text{ cm}}{1 \text{ min}} = 30$ cm/min

Height of the wall after 40 min $= \frac{30 \text{ cm}}{1 \text{ min}} \times 40 \text{ min} = 1200$ cm

Let x be the height of wall, then $\frac{3}{4}x = 1200 \text{ cm} \to x = \frac{4 \times 1200}{3} \to x = 1600 \text{ cm} = 16$ m

16)   *Choice A is correct*

$$\frac{(7+5)^2}{4} + 5 = \frac{(12)^2}{4} + 5 = \frac{144}{4} + 5 = 36 + 5 = 41$$

17)   *Choice E is correct*

$y = 4ab + 3b^3$

Plug in the values of a and b in the equation: $a = 2$ and $b = 3$

$y = 4\,(2)\,(3) + 3\,(3)^3 = 24 + 3(27) = 24 + 81 = 105$

18)   *Choice A is correct*

$\frac{2}{3} \cong 0.67$ $\frac{5}{7} \cong 0.71$ $\frac{8}{11} \cong 0.73$ $\frac{3}{4} = 0.75$

19)   *Choice C is correct*

Use the formula of the area of circles.

Area $= \pi r^2 \Rightarrow 64\,\pi = \pi r^2 \Rightarrow 64 = r^2 \Rightarrow r = 8$

Radius of the circle is 8. Now, use the circumference formula:

Circumference $= 2\pi r = 2\pi\,(8) = 16\,\pi$

20) Choice C is correct

x is the number of all sales profit and 2% of it is:

$2\% \times x = 0.02x$

Employee's revenue: $0.02x + 7000$

21) Choice D is correct

$0.6x = (0.3) \times 20 \to x = 10 \to (x + 5)^2 = (10 + 5)^2 = (15)^2 = 225$

22) Choice C is correct

Prime factorizing of 36= $2 \times 2 \times 3 \times 3$

Prime factorizing of 54= $2 \times 3 \times 3 \times 3$

GCF= $2 \times 3 \times 3 = 18$

23) Choice B is correct

$\frac{2}{5}$ Of 120= $\frac{2}{5} \times 120 = 48$

$\frac{1}{4}$ Of 48 = $\frac{1}{4} \times 48 = 12$

24) Choice E is correct

The sum of all angles in a quadrilateral is 360 degrees.

Let x be the smallest angle in the quadrilateral. Then the angles are:

$x, 2x, 2x, 5x$

$x + 2x + 2x + 5x = 360 \to 10x = 360 \to x = 36$

The angles in the quadrilateral are: 36°, 72°, 72°, and 180°

25) Choice C is correct

Length of the rectangle is: $\frac{5}{4} \times 16 = 20$

Perimeter of rectangle is: $2 \times (20 + 16) = 72$

"Effortless Math Education" Publications

Effortless Math authors' team strives to prepare and publish the best quality SSAT Mathematics learning resources to make learning Math easier for all. We hope that our publications help you learn Math in an effective way and prepare for the SSAT test.

We all in Effortless Math wish you good luck and successful studies!

Effortless Math Authors

Online Math Lessons

Enjoy interactive Math lessons online

with the best Math teachers

Online Math learning that's effective, affordable, flexible, and fun

Learn Math wherever you want; when you want

Ultimate flexibility. You can now learn Math online, enjoy high quality engaging lessons no matter where in the world you are. It's affordable too.

Learn Math with one-on-one classes

We provide one-on-one Math tutoring online. We believe that one-to-one tutoring is the most effective way to learn Math.

Qualified Math tutors

Working with the best Math tutors in the world is the key to success! Our tutors give you the support and motivation you need to succeed with a personal touch.

Online Math Lessons

It's easy! Here's how it works.

1- Request a FREE introductory session.

2- Meet a Math tutor online.

3- Start Learning Math in Minutes.

Send Email to: info@EffortlessMath.com

Made in the USA
Middletown, DE
20 November 2018